# Derailing the Constitution:
## The Undermining of American Federalism

# Derailing the Constitution

## The Undermining of
## American Federalism

*edited by*
## Edward B. McLean

**Intercollegiate Studies Institute**
*Bryn Mawr, Pennsylvania*

Copyright ©1995 by the Intercollegiate Studies Institute

All rights reserved. No part of this publication may be repro-
duced or transmitted in any form or by any means, electronic or
mechanical, including photocopy, or any information storage
and retrieval system now known or to be invented, without
permission in writing from the publisher, except by a reviewer
who wishes to quote brief passages in connection with a review
written for inclusion in a magazine, newspaper, or broadcast.

Library of Congress Catalog Card Number
94-73312


ISBN 1-882926-06-4


Published in the United States by:

Intercollegiate Studies Institute
14 South Bryn Mawr Avenue
Bryn Mawr, PA 19010


Manufactured in the United States of America

# Contents

# Introduction

Edward B. McLean

The current debate surrounding the role of the Supreme Court of the United States and the justifications for its decisions come down quite simply to the issue of whether or not there is a constitution which defines, limits, and controls the operation of the national government. The questions raised pertain to all three branches of the national government—executive, legislative, and judicial. The focus of these essays is primarily on the role of the Judiciary in its interpretation of the Constitution.

The "liberal" mode—whether we call it interpretivist, loose construction, or whatever—is not to be criticized if there is *not* a constitution which defines, limits, and controls the operation of the national government. The outlook from which this liberal mode operates considers *only* the *power* of the national government, and assumes that this power is to be exercised throughout an empire, with the only restraints on its application being those that stem from prudence, expediency, or insufficient power. Glaringly absent from this liberal formulation is a sense of restraint that flows from *any* external or transcendent principle. To the liberal mind there is not a permanent or identifiable constitutional design that is to be respected, preserved, or considered in order to control governmental power. The momentum of liberalism's drive for concentration, centralization, and mobilization of power necessarily and logically rejects concepts of limitation and control. "Politics" in the liberal mode operates with its own logic for the expansion, centralization, and mobilization of power. Concepts of limitation are alien to the liberal notion of politics, the outcomes of which are the distribution of rewards and the imposition of costs which are as expansive as the human imagination. Mobilization of power behind some distributive scheme is the primary object of politics; success in the electoral process is the only sought after end in politics; "principle" is purely a rhetorical device employed to mask the unlimited drive for power and control; and the Constitution is a document of no import or value to those who view politics in this fashion.

The Founding Fathers understood the nature of politics better. They comprehended its generating forces and the logic of its operation. Consequently, they specifically sought, in drafting and adopting the Constitution, to provide a restraint on the momentum of politics; to thwart its logic of operation; and to make impotent its generative power. They did so in two ways: (1) by institutional design, and (2) by emphasizing the need for principled limitation. The initial persuasion of the states to join the federation was the security anchored in the Constitution— to divide power at the national level through the separation of powers; to provide dual *sovereignty* between the national government and the respective states; and to base governance on the principle of identified and identifiable limitation.

The separation of powers at the national level was designed to fragment power, by providing institutional checks which were specifically designed to thwart the concentration of power in any one or more branches of the national government. The Founding Fathers were not carried away by the casuistical argument of "mixed functions." Quite the contrary, they viewed the essential nature of the national government as being one where specific functions were assigned and *assignable* to specific branches of that national government. Because these functions were different, the logic of checks and balances could work.

Most assuredly the Founders did not intend nor did they foresee the lock-step arrangement between the legislature, the courts, and the executive that has characterized national governmental power and its exercise over the past half century. The unity of design and desire by the functionaries of the national government today is clearly evidenced in the assault on the Constitution that has occurred and is occurring by all of the branches of the national government and their perverse and alarming willingness to destroy the constitutional design. The enormity of the plundering operation conducted under the guise of constitutional exercise of power is astonishing. Such mobilization, concentration, and centralization of power cannot be interpreted as part of the original design of the Constitution. The specificity of the beneficiaries and the losers, whose condition is determined by the outcome of the operation of this centralized power, cannot be justified by the principles that undergirded the Constitution at its founding, nor can they be conceived to have been the intended result of the separation of powers. The record of the national government's motives, the ends it pursues, and the means it adopts provide an astonishing commentary on the death of the Constitution. What those in the national government have in common is their willful assault on the federal scheme. Madison in *Federalist* Number Ten may have "gotten it right" in the eighteenth century about the nature of faction being a danger only in the states. What he did not foresee was that the cautionary statements he made regarding the danger of faction would become an even more pressing danger to the constitutional scheme with the destruction of an effective doctrine of separation of powers, the emergence of strong centralized and concentrated imperial national government, and the slow and cruel execution of the federal scheme of government.

The Constitution clearly specifies and limits the powers of the national government. Further, it clearly and specifically states what limitations on the state governments are embodied in the Constitution; finally, with clarity it states that whatever is not specified as a power of the national government, and is not prohibited to the states, is reserved to the states or the people through the amendatory process. No one in honesty can deny this fundamental truth about the language of the Constitution and the principles that support it. American constitutional history, however, is characterized by a long and purposeful attack on this very fundamental core of the constitutional order. The record clearly reveals the seizure and expansion of power by the imperial national government, and the diminution of the states' powers to serve and protect their citizens.

The concentration, centralization, and mobilization of power at the national level has almost completely destroyed the capacity of the states to serve their citizens effectively, and in conformance with the prescriptions of the Constitution. In effect, the constitutional revolution carried off by officialdom in Washington, D.C., has stripped the states of their powers, which were designed to be protected by the Constitution. States are no longer effectively able to protect the health, morals, and safety of their citizens. Rather, their citizens are subject to the dictates of the national government and are "objects" of its power. This frightful situation is not made less so by pointing to the fact that some have had their life conditions improved by the use of unconstitutional national power. Even Mussolini made the trains run on time. Sheer chance and good fortune guarantee some degree of success in carrying forward "reform" and "revision." The sheer volume and intensity of the application of power by the national government masks the absolute incapacity of national, centralized, and unconstitutional government to deal constructively or realistically with the problems faced on a day-to-day basis by the citizenry of the nation. What propels this dismal ineffectiveness is the self-generating power of national politics, and the perpetual addition of new "programs" to correct the new problems and crises created by those "programs" which preceded them. The delusional behavior of the United States Congress is matched by the delusional behavior of the judicial and the executive branches of government. The latter particularly is prone to exacerbating the decay of the American Republic. The bureaucracy of the executive branch, like any bureaucracy, has only one generative force, and that is expansion—expansion of program and control. To assume that any bureaucracy is content to solve a problem is to ignore the fundamental nature of the bureaucrat and the bureau he serves. The bureaucrat's quest for the expansion of his power is buoyed up by the legislature's desire to "manage" problems, not solve them. This fantasy world of the national legislature and the executive is not diminished or held in check by the federal courts. Rather, the Supreme Court is as much of the problem as the legislature and the executive. Indeed they all are "co-conspirators" in the process of furthering the nearly completed destruction of the federal scheme.

If there is to be a reconstitution of the constitutional scheme, one must consider from whence such reconstruction should come. It is evident that the reconstitution cannot come from or through the political process. The inner logic of American electoral politics prohibits such a reconstitution. Constitutional governance requires that the political process be limited in scope—a notion not entertained by *any* national political figure. In addition, constitutional governance requires not merely that the power of the national state be limited in terms of scope, but also in terms of what de Jouvenal calls intensity, *i.e.*, the degree to which it can penetrate into the affairs of men in their personal lives, their voluntary relations with their fellows, the use and transference of their property, and their sense of morality, safety, and health. The nature of the political process rejects this limitation on national power. The generative force of the political process expands the power exercised by the national state over the lives, properties, destinies, and values of the public it dominates. Even if there were persons of good will involved in this process, they would find themselves powerless to operate within it without the sacrifice of all principle based on the need for "compromise." This euphemistically denominated "pragmatism" inevitably leads to collusion in the drive of national governmental power to dominate the lives of the citizens and to determine their affairs, values, abilities, and opportunities. What Hayek calls the "playball of interests" constitutes the only rule in the political process. If politicians are not held to account for their repeated violations of the Constitution, this can only mean that such limitations are ineffective. The process, which more and more comes to be dominated by the least ethical individuals, cannot find the internal strength or motive to cease its destruction of the constitutional scheme. The Constitution, instead of operating as a restraint on such exercises of power, becomes a rhetorical symbol to justify such an exercise. Nothing in the nature of the political process even suggests limitation. Consequently, if the actors in this process feel no restraint, they will exercise none. The political process, however, is not the only cause of the destruction of the constitutional scheme. The inattentiveness and greed of the population at large feeds the system. The myth of the "service state," which has become for most Americans the operative premise they entertain about the role of politics, generates a real enthusiasm for the state's expansion in scope and intensity. While a "yeoman farmer" may decry the redistributions of wealth to the indigent mother, he will accept and encourage redistribution of such wealth in exchange for wheat subsidies, or milk subsidies. The solid, self-reliant banker may decry the subsidies given to the farmer as illustrative of unwarranted redistribution, but will accept and encourage redistribution of the state in favor of poorly managed, if not criminally mismanaged, savings and loan institutions.

Such a list of contradictions could fill a volume. What they all point to, however, is the American citizenry's fatal misunderstanding about the purpose of political order, the nature of constitutional government, and most particularly the nature of the federal scheme. Such a corrupted view among the public, joined with the nature of the political process, constitutes a malevolent alliance that propels the society toward totalitarianism. Even though this may not be the anticipated or desired objective of anyone, such action and inaction almost assures such an outcome.

Thus, if reconstitution cannot come from the political process, or popular sentiment, then from whence can it come? The most likely answer is the courts themselves. Even though the federal courts particularly have been major actors in the destruction of the constitutional order, the possibility of reconstitution lies in their action. Whether this is probable or not depends on whether the federal courts will develop bases for their actions which are grounded in reason, logic, and the Constitution. Indeed, only if judges can avoid the quagmire of passion that so intensely affects the political process will this be possible. Judges need to recapture a sense of first principles about their profession and their occupation. First of all, they must recall that the law with which the courts deal is not some amorphous collection of sayings, rules, standards, and concepts which can be molded at will to bring about a predetermined conclusion or outcome. Even though the law, as it currently is taught in most law schools of the land, conveys this notion, the purifying effect of law practice tends to mitigate the damage done to lawyers by their legal education. The operation of the law is tied intimately, if not inseparably, to the content and scope of legal philosophy. Therefore, essays directed at clarifying the understanding of the nature of constitutional philosophy constitute mighty weapons in any effort to reconstitute the Constitution. However, the chaff must be separated from the wheat. Law journals published at most law schools today are the chaff. The wheat is to be found in such a collection of essays as are assembled here.

These are essays which seek a truthful and candid examination of the Constitution. They are not written to promote someone's career, for each contributor to this collection has already established himself as a leader in the law. Examination of the law should be done from multiple sources and fortunately these essays are written by persons with diverse backgrounds and professional callings. Improvement and clarification of the law has resulted from the efforts of theologians, laymen, ethicists, judges, and lawyers. The modern day mega-law school is a recent and unfortunate phenomenon. Law schools *per se* exhibit the same weaknesses of the political process, or institutionalized bureaucracies, as do national governments. The dominant purposes of legal training usually has little to do with the understanding or operation of the law. Other, more valued matters dominate the operation of most law schools, such as building expansion (a highly subjective game of prestige building in competition with each other), abstract and nonsensical legal schemes of thought (such as critical legal studies), and appropriations for improved faculty salaries, research grants, library acquisitions, etc. None of this has much to do with casting light on the complex questions of legal procedure, rules of evidence, or the practice of law. Yet the influence of such institutions has come to dominate the legal profession, and the legal profession has, almost wholesale, turned over its direction, composition, and soul to law school faculties, which are composed, in the most part, of persons who have never practiced law.

This perverse and illogical development is part of the problem addressed in these essays, *i.e.*, from whence do lawyers derive their ideas about the nature of the Constitution? The answer is, unfortunately, from their law professors, who, in large measure, obtain their ideas in turn from the writings of other law professors, whose understanding of the Constitution, is, to say the least, inadequate and incomplete. Fortunately, there are others who can and do contribute to the dialogue about the Constitution. Each of the essays contained in this volume were lectures delivered either at the Federalist Society Program, organized and directed by Ian McLean at the Indiana University School of Law in Bloomington on October 17 and 18, 1987, or in the Goodrich Lecture Series at Wabash College during the 1987-1988 academic year. Each addresses the nature of the Constitution, and points to the error of contemporary thinking about the Constitution.

Forrest McDonald's essay "I Have Seen the Past and It Works" provides the fitting point of departure for the lectures in this volume. McDonald correctly points out that the Constitution presupposes certain external institutional arrangements, a specific understanding of the nature of man and society, and what is possible and desirable in the realm of government. McDonald clearly illuminates what these understandings were for those who founded the American Republic. Their understanding led them to spell out in the Constitution clear and unequivocal limitations on the powers of the national government. The federal structure reflected the Founders' recognition of the importance of letting those who would live under governmental decisions be close to the institutions of government that would make them. The Founders also understood the nature of man—his flaws and imperfectibility—and assumed that government would have to deal with this critical factor. In addition, the Founders recognized that those who would take over the helm of government would seek to use that governmental power and prestige for their own aggrandizement. Because men are driven by the desire for profit and power and will not hesitate to use government to achieve them, it is essential to limit the powers of government. These sensible and helpful formulae have been abandoned in the modern era. As McDonald points out, government has metastasized to the extent that it has practically destroyed the original scheme of government. The fact that a few liberties remain, according to McDonald, is a result of the institutionalized incompetence of those who govern and not a desire to preserve such liberties. As he wryly comments, we are fortunate in that we get only a fraction of the government we pay for.

The modern mind, McDonald observes, having become infatuated with "science," presumes that if one cannot think "scientifically" about matters, then one cannot think about them at all. There is a critical difference between what this mindset believes and what the men of the eighteenth century considered the value of this "formulaic" thinking. This mode of thought, they recognized, was usable for some things, but *not* for questions concerning men and society. The Founders' wisdom regarding morality, the nature of government, the nature of man, and the institutional requisites for a wholesome political order embody the ideas which should be used by modern man. The infatuation of the modern mind with Lockean notions, the impoverished thought of Marx and Freud, all have contributed to American decline which is marked by luxury, corruption, moral relativism, and the notion of progress. All of these stand in stark contrast to the perceptivity and common sense of the Founders. McDonald urges a reformulation of the way in which we think about the Constitution, the conclusions we seek, and the values we endorse. These matters would be better addressed if we adopted the wisdom and prudence of the Founders of the Republic. The ease with which modern men accept false ideals, the easy rejection of moral considerations, the contemporary misunderstanding about man's nature and his imperfectibility, and the rejection of institutional designs which are capable of preserving free men have all led to the deplorable state of government in contemporary American society.

McDonald's essay underscores the specific intention of the Founders in adopting a federal scheme. Justice Donnelly's examination of the decay of the constitutional federal scheme continues this theme. As Justice Donnelly points out, the prevailing view at the time of the ratification of the Constitution was that the national government had only a few, well-defined powers and that the Tenth Amendment reserved all those that had not been delegated to the national government to the states, which were the creators of the federal scheme. A short fifty years ago the Tenth Amendment was considered impregnable. Today it is considered obsolete. Justice Donnelly identifies the three land-mark events which resulted in this constitutional revolution. The first of these was the adoption of the Seventeenth Amendment, which provided for the direct election of United States Senators. The second occurred on September 29, 1958, when the Supreme Court of the United States, in *Cooper v. Aaron*, 358 U.S. 1 (1958), declared that its decisions are "the supreme law of the land." This fiat and unconstitutional judgment of the Court has resulted in a series of decisions that have abrogated state laws without constitutional justification and redesigned the United States government to permit social policy to be determined by persons who are not held accountable for their decisions by the electorate. The third occurred on February 19, 1985, when the Supreme Court virtually excised the Tenth Amendment from the United States Constitution, in *Garcia v. San Antonio Metropolitan Transit Authority*, 469 U.S. 528 (1985). In this case the Court rejected what it contemptuously called the "traditional governmental functions" consigned to the states by the Tenth Amendment.

Justice Donnelly points out that the activism of the Supreme Court, in its supervision and destruction of state law, is paralleled by its reluctance to interfere with the actions of the national government. This development in Court attitude reverses the constitutional powers and responsibilities which were intended by the Framers of the Constitution and those who obtained the ratification of the Fourteenth Amendment. The developments which have flowed from these three watershed events have culminated in the establishment of " . . . a model outside the

Constitution. In this new formulation the Supreme Court of the United States (1) ... will sit as a Council of Revision over the States ... (2) the Court will no longer defend the States against the actions taken by Congress under the aegis of the Commerce Clause; and (3) if Congress should undertake to address the parameters of the Fourteenth Amendment, the Court will decide if its articulations are *right* and *good*."

Justice Donnelly, in a measured response to this series of developments, states his concern about the reformulation of the Constitution without consultation with the people. His essay is a profoundly important outline of the true nature of the crisis that affects our constitutional scheme of government. We have witnessed, in a scarce fifty years, a *radical* transformation of the structural design of the system of governance that was established to define and assign the respective powers of the dual sovereignties present in the American scheme. Most important in considering this fateful occurrence is Justice Donnelly's concern for the disappearance, for all intents and purposes, of the role of the citizenry and the states in the reformulation of the new constitutional form under which we live. Justice Donnelly clearly establishes the support for his conclusion that "[t]he people, not the Court, should articulate the moral sense of abstract principles of just government in contemporary circumstances."

Professor William B. Allen provides an innovative and clarifying argument regarding the "interpretivist" and "noninterpretivist" constitutional debate. He distinguishes between original intent *ab initio* and *ab principo*. The current debate that focuses on the argument of original intent *ab initio*, Professor Allen states, poses little threat to the contemporary political and legal order, since there is nothing that is principled in such an argument that could be used to combat current thinking which seeks to destroy the Constitution. On the other hand, the argument of original intent *ab principo* compels attention be given to the fundamental problem that lies at the base of this debate, namely, the entire issue of legitimacy of the Court's behavior and constitutional interpretation. The debate surrounding the Constitution today raises the same issue as that posed by the Court's actions in the era immediately preceding the War between the States, which ignored the fact that the determination of what is constitutional lies with the populace, and not with the Court. Non-interpretivists err when they do not focus on the real issue, *i.e.*, the *principles* which undergird the Constitution. These principles inhere in the Constitution and *cannot* be removed by judicial fiat. The ultimate remedy lies in the public's reaction to the series of illegitimate decisions and misreadings of the Constitution that come from the Supreme Court. Obviously, a series of remedies for this misapplication and misinterpretation of the Constitution are available. These remedies range from the election of a President who would not give effect to court decisions, to active revolution. One need only look at the success of the civil rights activists of the 1960s to see with clarity the correctness of Professor Allen's view. What supported such activism primarily was that its appeals were predicated on the original intent of the Constitution *ab principo*, and not intent *ab initio*. Had their aspirations been predicated on the latter, little legitimacy could have been extended to their desire for the removal of legislative enactments which were accomplished with procedural correctness. The appeal to the public at large found receptivity, because it was based on the foundation discussed in Professor Allen's timely and important essay. As disquieting as it may seem, it may only be revolutionary activity which can restore constitutional government in this country.

Justice Richard Neely's essay strikes a discordant note in the debate regarding federalism. According to Justice Neely, most of the debate over the issue of federalism is academic and unimportant. This conclusion stems from his argument that there are three broad perspectives to be employed in evaluating federalism. These perspectives are historical federalism, result-oriented federalism, and practical federalism.

Neely believes that nothing of merit can be found in the historical justification of federalism. The federal scheme which was adopted over two hundred years ago has been displaced and destroyed by intervening events, not the least of which are the Civil War and the adoption of the Thirteenth and Fourteenth Amendments. According to Justice Neely, America's population at large places most of its trust and confidence in the national government. Consequently, whatever state power remains is for convenience, and is not preserved because of constitutional requirement.

Result-oriented federalism, Justice Neely argues, is the doctrine of federalism that receives the most "die hard" political support. This particular doctrine is internally inconsistent, for often supporters of a "pure" federalism in one area will call for national governmental assistance and regulation in another. Result-oriented federalism, Justice Neely concludes, is simply a matter of political muscle combined with some quick conclusions about whose ox is being gored. Consequently, it is of enormous practical concern, but unworthy of being taken seriously as being based on any legal principle, and certainly cannot provide for any logically coherent means of interpreting the Constitution.

Practical federalism, Neely feels, deserves both respect and understanding. One of the primary benefits that flows from it is the competition that exists between state governments in terms of development, economic distribution, and preserving opportunities for initiative. In addition, the efficiency of government in delivering governmental services at all levels is enhanced by federalism viewed in this fashion. The real merits of practical federalism, Neely feels, cannot be denied. Practical federalism does not require that theoretical solutions be found for practical problems. Consequently, it can effectively address such issues as where problems can be most efficiently and effectively handled—

at the national or local level.

In Justice Neely's opinion, the singular most important task for the courts is to assure that continued national governmental intrusions into the affairs of the states is compelled for some good and substantive reason, and not merely an exercise of power by the national government, which has the means to control resources and personnel. The preservation of practical federalism is not an exercise in theory, but rather an exercise in pragmatic, economic, sociological, and political analysis that deals with issues on a case-by-case basis. According to Neely, the strength of America's constitutional order stems from the rejection of rigid theoretical constitutional arguments. The success of the American experience in government stems from the ascendancy of practical federalism.

Professor William F. Harvey's lecture—"The Life and Death of the Fourteenth Amendment and Its Federalism: Requiem for a Heavyweight"—starts with the proposition that the Constitution is to be praised, not the Supreme Court. The Constitution at its origin was designed to bring into being a scheme of governance that would limit state power, and would deny to anyone the ability to rule absolutely over others. This ideal of government formed the foundation for the adoption of the Fourteenth Amendment's "Privileges and Immunities" Clause. This provision made two major changes in the existing constitutional scheme: (1) It extended the elements of liberty to all persons, and (2) it considered the elements of liberty in the Privileges and Immunities Clause to be absolute. The Privileges and Immunities Clause was designed to assure that there would be no discrimination in the protection of the civil rights or immunities of citizens; that every person should be guaranteed the right to contract; that every person should be able to institute and defend in suits at law; that all could hold and convey real estate; that everyone would be able to engage in an occupation of his choosing; and everyone could claim the protection of the writ of *habeas corpus*. It also intended that no exercise of state power could legitimately intrude on these guaranteed liberties.

The Supreme Court's misreading and misinterpretation of the Privileges and Immunities Clause, Professor Harvey shows, set the stage for "Jim Crow" legislation and the long and desultory history of racial discrimination in the American Republic. This result was directly attributed to the activism and disregard of the original intent of the Constitution by the Supreme Court. The men serving on the Court at the time reflected in their decision the errors of constitutional judgment that still affect the Court today. They did not comprehend the intention of the Constitution, they did not understand that rights and liberties are not conditional gifts from government, and they did not understand the great mission of the Constitution to limit state power in specific and determinate ways in order that liberty might be preserved. Professor Harvey cogently argues that the law issued by the Court may depend on the personnel of the Court, but that the Constitution does not and should not depend on this factor. The tragedy of the Fourteenth Amendment's fate at the hands of the Supreme Court was not that it was tried and found wanting, but rather that it was not tried at all.

Judge Pasco Bowman's address deals with the importance of the doctrine of the separation of powers in the Constitution, the treatment this doctrine has received from the Supreme Court of the United States, and the current state or significance of that doctrine in American Constitutional Law.

Three concerns dominated the Founding Fathers' deliberations and decisions regarding the design of the new constitution. First, the inadequate powers of the central government under the Articles of Confederation; second, their fear of established, strong, central authority; and, third, their concern regarding the potential for abuse in any arrangement where *too* much power is concentrated in the same hands. The Founding Fathers were impressed with parts of the British experiment with mixed government and Montesquieu's theory of separation of powers. This doctrine was operative in several state constitutions, and, as Judge Bowman points out, although the doctrine is not explicitly mentioned in the Constitution of the United States, it is incorporated through the provisions for the establishment of the three departments of the government—legislative, executive, and judicial. Indeed, as Judge Bowman goes on to say, the constitutional provisions that established these three branches speak of such grants in *exclusive* terms, *i.e.*, each branch is granted *all* of the power in its respective field. The importance the Founding Fathers attached to assuring that power would not be concentrated is underscored by their decision to create two coordinate houses in the legislature, the specific limitations they placed on the scope of legislative power, and specific prohibitions on the exercise of certain powers by the national government. Finally, the Constitution provides that all of those powers not specifically given to the national government are reserved to the states.

The constitutional design clearly was intended to create a limited national government. The powers vested in the national government were divided among three branches, and the Constitution created a *federal* scheme of government. One of the most important factors in the design of the federal system was the assurance that most of the powers of government would be reserved to the states. In sum, the intent of the constitutional design was to create a system of government of law and not men. The separation of powers doctrine was intended to assure this result and to secure liberty for the citizens of a nation under a limited government.

In light of the Founders' original intention, Judge Bowman poses the question of whether the system has been successfully preserved. His answer is a "qualified yes." The institutional structure has been largely preserved. Nonetheless, Judge Bowman goes on to point to those disturbing developments which threaten the preservation of the separation of powers as a vital element of constitutional government.

The first of these developments is a result of the expansive view that has been given the enumerated powers in Article I. This expansive view has resulted in the unwarranted expansion of national governmental power into the affairs of the states and the lives of their individual citizens. The scope and intensity of these powers far exceeds anything envisioned by the Framers of the Constitution.

Second, Judge Bowman feels that the Framers would be surprised at the extended and broadened conception the Supreme Court has of its jurisdiction. This expanded view has enabled the Court to encroach on both the powers of the states and the other branches of the national government.

The phenomenal growth of administrative power at the national level, with the development of agencies that wield extensive and largely uncontrollable power over the lives and destinies of American citizens, reflects this development. Even though such agencies are subject to judicial scrutiny, their very size and the scope of their control creates an element of government that is antithetical and hostile to the Constitution's doctrine of separation of powers.

Judge Bowman points to the necessary task that remains to be accomplished by those who appreciate the intention of constitutional government that is designed to preserve the separation of powers and individual liberty. Preservation of this element of constitutional government would assure a government of laws and not men.

Dr. Allan Carlson's lecture deals with "The Family and the Constitution." Carlson maintains that the Constitution of the United States, unlike other constitutions of the Western world, does not touch on the institutions of family and marriage. The Founders of the Republic believed that the protection of and decisions related to the family would be left to the states, and thus would be protected from domination by the national government.

According to Carlson, the family was characterized by five qualities at the end of the eighteenth century. First, the family was the primary economic unit of society. Families were largely self-sufficient and constituted the focus of all of their members' economic activities. Second, families reflected the strong religious and ethnic unity that was characteristic of most of American life. Third, the identity and unity of the family was centered directly on the land. Fourth, there was a premium placed on large, cohesive families. Fifth, families were characterized by the binding power of inter-generational ties. Thus, families constituted the primary focus of eighteenth–century American economic and social existence, and the Founders believed that families were the major source of an orderly and free society.

According to Carlson, there has been an unending assault directed against the American family since the 1840s. The first direct assault was in the form of the "reform school" movement in the 1830s. This movement sought to take children from parents who were considered unequal to the task of providing proper education for their children, or who were "unworthy" parents. The underlying justification for this direct assault on the integrity and autonomy of the family institution resulted in the judicially created doctrine of *parens patriae.*

The second assault came from the creation of the public school system and compulsory education. Motivated by a desire to "socialize" immigrants, foster religious unitarianism, and reinforce political liberalism, this educational movement resulted in a direct and unapologetic attack on the very notion of the family institution. Not only did this educational system replace the family as the primary institution for the formation of the young, but it had a devastating effect on the family as an economic unit.

The twentieth century's emphasis on individualism, the concept of the welfare state, and the unlimited ability and willingness of the national government to replace state governmental functions at will have stripped the family of its most secure protections and destroyed its role in the development and maintenance of an orderly and free society. The destructive effect of these developments has been enhanced by actions of the national government. Among these are the Supreme Court's radical interpretation of what families are, the denial of the concept of family as an institution within which unique and valuable relationships exist that are anterior to state power, and the national legislature's tax policies, which have all but destroyed the family as a viable economic institution. These additional assaults may result in the very extinction of the institution of the family.

Carlson feels that remedial action can be taken that would preserve and protect the family. First, he urges reform of the tax laws in order to affirm the value of marriage and children. Second, he proposes development of housing policies that would restore home ownership and the linkage of the family to the land. Third, he encourages reforming the nation's fiscal policies in order to encourage the return of economic activities to the home.

As Carlson warns, the survival of liberty and constitutional government may well depend on the ability of the American public to restrain state power and to restore families to their role as *the* fundamental institution in society.

Carlson's paper underscores how essential it is to restore the federal scheme of government embodied in our Constitution. There is no constitutionally permissible basis for the national government to control and direct families. The Constitution specifically delimits the powers of the national government, and those specific powers do not include its authority to develop policy and tax programs designed to control or destroy the family. What legal direction and control of families that are required should be restored to the states, and the usurpations of the national government should be unmasked for what they are and stripped from the numerous unconstitutional powers now wielded by national government.

In his essay "The Constitution: The Guarantor of Religion," Professor Charles Rice examines the Supreme Court's recent departure from any recognizable constitutional principle in its treatment of the First Amendment and the question of the relationship of religion to the state. As Rice points out, the First Amendment's prohibition of the establishment of a religion is subordinate to the major purpose of that amendment—the protection of the free exercise of religion. The Court's proper reading of the First Amendment was reflected in its early history. In addition, the national legislature and the executive also understood that the Founders intended that the Constitution was expected to promote Christianity, or at least theism. Consequently, the constitutional system worked well as long as the people of the United States adhered to Christianity, and as long as they recognized that the general propositions of Christian reading of natural law were implicit in the Constitution. As this cohesive understanding of the close relationship between Christianity and the Constitution eroded, it was accelerated and accentuated by the insistent behavior of the Court to develop a stance that is hostile to Christianity and to theism. The contemporary Court has, in defiance of the specific constitutional prohibition against it, established a formal, identifiable state religion—agnosticism. Court decisions specifically prohibit state agencies—particularly schools—from affirming theism, or teaching atheism. What the court does insist on is the fostering of an official stance of agnostic secularism. The Court has developed bizarre and casuistical tests to mask its hostility to the Constitution and religion.

Rice cogently argues and demonstrates that the Founding Fathers' understanding of the Constitution served as a guarantor of religion—particularly Christianity. They understood fully the interconnection between religious belief and civic virtue and evidenced this understanding in their actions and statements. Their concern was to prevent the national government from legislating any establishment of religion or prohibiting the free exercise of religion. Their specific intention in prohibiting the national government from establishing a religion was to assure that *all* matters related to religion would be exclusively and unrestrictedly handled by state governments. As Professor Rice concludes, the establishment clause was not intended as a means of protecting personal liberty. Rather, it was designed to delimit and delineate the jurisdictional spheres of the national and state governments. The Supreme Court's seizure of power, in violation of the Constitution, has distorted the role of federalism and the Constitution. Because of this usurpation by the Court, generations of children are programmed in public schools to assume that there are no standards higher than those enunciated by the State. The national state, under the prompting of the Supreme Court, commands that the youth of this nation be subjected to the dictate that *all* sensitive matters—homosexuality, abortion, criminal license—be approached in a non-judgmental manner. The ultimate cost to the Republic from this type of distortion and abandonment of the Constitution are yet to be reckoned.

These essays provide but a start on the enormous task of restoring the constitutional form of government in this country. The usurpation of power and prerogative by functionaries in Washington, D.C., is dangerous and inconsistent with constitutional government. The mask of rhetoric that comes from the liberal mindset, which glories in this centralization and concentration of power in violation of the Constitution, should be attacked vigorously and unapologetically by all persons of good will in this nation. These essays constitute an important step in the recognition and correction of our current state of affairs. As long as there are persons who can address the nature of these problems there is hope.

America has become a nation ruled by a new and malignant form of orthodoxy—an orthodoxy that is enunciated from a centralized and concentrated source of power in the national government. No reading of the Constitution can justify this or even rationalize it. The orthodox opinions that are compelled to be accepted run counter to the fundamental tenets of the Christian faith or any doctrine of theism. It would be a different matter if this orthodoxy were a product of the effective influence of private organizations that had persuaded a populace to endorse their views. Such is not the case. In direct contravention of the Constitution, such orthodoxy is supported, fostered, and protected by an imperial national government. This book points to the many areas of American life where this is the case. The Constitution was designed specifically to keep this from happening, and one can only conclude it can happen because the Constitution has been abandoned by the Court, the national legislature, and the national executive. If constitutional governance is to be restored it must acknowledge this and begin the great task of repair. It is to this end that these essays are directed.

# I Have Seen the Past and It Works

## Forrest McDonald

During the Great Depression of the 1930s, a number of left-wing intellectuals went from the United States to the Soviet Union and returned with the glib announcement, "I have seen the future and it works." My thesis here is the opposite: "I have seen the past and it works." What follows is an effort to elaborate and justify that proposition, beginning with the drafting of the American Constitution in 1787.

Now, there are a number of things about the founding of the American constitutional order that are commonly missed because students of the Constitution tend to overlook the crucial fact that the Framers put more into it than is made quite explicit in the text. That is to say, the Constitution presupposes certain external institutional arrangements, and it presupposes as well an understanding about the nature of man and society and about what, in the realm of government, is possible and desirable.

The institutional presuppositions are the most evident, inasmuch as they largely turn upon the prior existence of the several states that composed the federal union. The most important of the institutional arrangements in the original system had to do with the organic structure of power. On the federal level, government had only such powers as were expressly delegated to it by the Constitution or could be reasonably inferred from the enumerated powers—and these were carefully limited, being confined essentially to interstate and international relations. (In the Constitutional Convention, Gouverneur Morris, ardent nationalist though he was, objected to the requirement that Congress meet at least once a year, his ground being that there would not be enough public business to warrant annual meetings.) But state and local governments, by contrast, would have all powers except the few that were expressly forbidden by the state constitutions and the somewhat larger number forbidden by the United States Constitution.

This scheme of things speaks a great deal about the Framers' understanding of the proper relationship of men, government, and society. To put it simply, they believed that the decisions that vitally affect people in their daily lives are most intelligently and safely made by those who feel the immediate consequences of the decisions. Specifically this meant state legislatures, militias, juries, towns, congregations, and heads of families.

Another key constitutional arrangement, likewise indicative of the Framers' beliefs, concerned elections. Though it is scarcely common knowledge even among specialists, the Constitution included both religious tests and property qualifications for those who elected members of Congress. The only officers of the federal government who were originally elected directly by the voters were members of the House of Representatives; senators were elected by the state legislatures. Article I, Section 2, paragraph 1 provides that the electors of the members of the House of Representatives "shall have the Qualifications requisite for Electors of the most numerous Branch of the State Legislature" in each state. To learn what that meant, we must turn to the state constitutions. We find there that every state imposed property qualifications for voters for the lower house of its legislature. We also find that almost every state required a belief in the Christian religion on the part of its legislators, who in turn elected United States Senators and, most commonly, presidential electors.

The reasons for such qualifications were, to Americans at the time, self-evident. The religious tests arose in part from the generally held belief that religion and morality were inseparable, but also from a more focused consideration. Voters, officials, jurors, and witnesses were repeatedly called upon to swear oaths of allegiance, fidelity, or truth-telling. The renowned Massachusetts minister Phillips Payson explained the necessity for such oaths by saying that "the fear and reverence of God, and the terrors of eternity are the most powerful restraints upon the minds of men; and hence it is of special importance in a free government."[1] In other words, if men believed in a future state of eternal rewards and punishments, their oaths were binding and credible—and if not, not.

As for property qualifications, there were two justifications. One was the stake-in-society principle: only those who paid taxes (which were commonly levied upon real property) could be justly consulted as to what taxes should be assessed; otherwise, the propertyless might tax those with property and appropriate the revenues for themselves. That would be outright theft. The other justification was the will theory: those who did not have their own means of support could not be deemed to have a will of their own; their votes could be bought by the wealthy—or, what was worse, by the government.

These ideas are fairly straightforward and readily demonstrable; another level of presupposition is more subtle. To do justice to the subject would require, minimally, a lengthy discourse upon Protestant theology, upon the common law, upon natural law, upon the philosophies of Montesquieu and John Locke, upon the *Commentaries* of Sir William Blackstone, upon the classical revival, upon English country-party ideology, and upon the Scottish Enlightenment—*plus* a summary of ancient, English, and American history as understood by the Framers. That being obviously beyond the scope of this essay, let me make bold to describe what I believe to be the essence—the bottom line, to employ a current vulgarism—of the Framers' view of human nature.

The bottom line is that the Framers believed in original sin, believed that man has a nature that is unchanging and base. They understood that man is inherently flawed, imperfect, and imperfectible, driven by selfish desires, reasonable only in the sense of being able to contrive means of satisfying the appetites. They were utterly contemptuous of abstract political theories based upon the notion that man and society are perfectible, or that evil can be eradicated, or that man can be taught to be other than self-interested, or that man is or can become a creature governed by reason, or that there can be a durable and free social order based upon equality, brotherhood, and virtue.

There was, for a time, a partial exception to those generalizations. In their enthusiasm for republicanism, *some* of the Patriots of 1776, especially those in New England and more especially those in Massachusetts, had embraced an extreme and doctrinaire version of that particular "ism." Puritanical classical republicanism, as espoused by the likes of John and Sam Adams, required almost superhuman virtue of the public and almost superhuman devotion to the welfare of the republic. A republic, John Adams wrote, could "only be supported by pure Religion or Austere Morals . . . . There must be a positive Passion for the public good [that is] Superior to all private Passions. Men must be ready . . . and be happy to sacrifice their private Pleasures, Passions and interests, . . . their private Friendships and dearest Connections, when they stand in Competition with the Rights of Society."[2]

Massachusetts and, in less Draconian ways, the other states attempted to force their citizens to behave in such a fashion for about a decade—until the whole enterprise was abruptly abandoned, early in 1787, in reaction to Shays' Rebellion and other manifestations of a lack of public virtue. Thenceforth, the nation's political leaders, as indicated, decided that it was more prudent to erect governmental institutions upon human baseness than upon human virtue.

Having said that, however, one must promptly enter a pair of demurrers. The first is that the United States was not—not yet—the society of acquisitive individualists that it would become in the nineteenth century. Americans did believe that private rights to life, liberty, and property were anterior to government and morally beyond its reach; but they also believed that society as such had rights and that these always took precedence over the rights of individuals. The thinking that underlay this order of priority was well grounded: organized society was necessary to the survival of the individual, but no individual was indispensable to the survival of society.

The other demurrer is more involved. Though man was imperfect and imperfectible, he was capable of nearly boundless improvement. The resolution of this seeming contradiction is to be found in the model of the human psyche that prevailed in the Western world in the eighteenth century. Ancient and medieval theories of the humours (blood, phlegm, choler or yellow bile, and melancholy or black bile) had been replaced by the theory of the passions. Passions meant not ardent emotions but drives for self-gratification. It was held that behavior was determined by one's particular mix of passions and that as one matured a single ruling passion normally tended to crowd out or overmaster the others. A few passions, such as love of glory or love of country, were noble, but most were ignoble, in keeping with man's base nature; and it was generally believed that men in public life were usually governed by either ambition or avarice, by the love of power or the love of money.

The possibility for self-improvement existed because the desire for the approval of one's peers and betters was understood as being among the most powerful of primary passions, ranking with craving for food and sex; and eighteenth-century Americans, aping the British, had devised strict codes for winning and expressing approval or disapproval. All social interactions, from

ballroom dancing to warfare, were stylized, ritualized, struc-
tured, mannered. For example, there were rules governing the
complementary closings of correspondence which indicated
precisely the nature of the relationship between the writer and
the addressee, and transgressing the boundaries of the relationship by using an improper closing could terminate the possibility
of future intercourse. Or consider the matter of handshaking.
When both parties used both hands, that was a mark of equality
and intimacy. Offering one hand each indicated cordial formal-
ity, tendering the index finger signified warm condescension,
offering the little finger indicated cold condescension.

Just how much these elaborate codes improved one's behavior
varied with the quality of persons whose approval or admiration
one sought. If one sought plaudits from the degenerates who
made up fashionable society in London, decadence, viciousness,
and profligacy were at a premium. For public men to seek the
applause of the rabble—to seek, that is, popularity—was equally
bad and fostered in such demagogues the worst of excesses, the
basest of traits. Far better was it to disregard both popular favor
and its opposite, the foolish advice that Polonius gave to Laertes,
"to thine own self be true," and instead to follow Joseph Addison's
advice and seek the approbation of the wise and the just—as
George Washington did throughout his adult life. And noblest
of all was it to try to win the approval of posterity, of generations
of discerning and virtuous people yet unborn.

The specific instrumentality through which one went about
the business of self-improvement arose from the concept of
character. The term *character* was rarely used in the eighteenth
century to refer to internal qualities, moral or otherwise. Rather,
in its most general usage it signified reputation: a man was said
to have a character for honesty or infidelity or rashness. But it
also, in polite society and among men in public life, meant a
persona that one deliberately selected and always wore: one
picked a role, like a part in a play, and self-consciously contrived

to act it unfailingly, ever to be in character. If one chose a character with which one was comfortable, and if one played it long enough and consistently enough, it became by degrees a "second nature," no longer self-conscious, that in practice superseded the first. One became, in other words, what one pretended to be.

The results, for good or ill, depended upon the character chosen and upon how well one acted it. Benjamin Franklin played a large and often contradictory array of characters during his long career, making it difficult for contemporaries and for historians to discern the true features of the man behind the masks. Thomas Jefferson essayed a succession of characters—he went so far as to change his handwriting several times—and though he played a number of them with consummate skill, he never found a public character with which he was comfortable. When he retired from the presidency, ending "the part which I have acted on the theatre of public life," he gladly resumed the "tranquil pursuits of science" for which nature had intended him.[3] George Washington, by contrast, played a progression of characters, each grander and nobler than the last, and played each so successfully that he ultimately transformed himself into a man of almost extrahuman virtue.

Let me try to summarize and bring to a focus what I have said so far. The Founding Fathers believed that men in government must be regarded as being driven by unbounded lust for power and profit. From this it followed, as James Madison teaches us in several *Federalist* essays, that the powers of government must be limited and defined, and that the greater the range of people affected by those powers, the more closely must the powers be limited and defined. It also followed that powers must be so distributed that people who are vested with them at any level have an interest in curbing the powers of all others.

Such arrangements were feasible because, and only because, Americans were capable of governing themselves by means external to what in Europe is called the state and what in the United States is called "the government." The most important means were three. The first was fear of divine retribution, in this world or in the next. The second was the pressure of society as an amorphous, undifferentiated, but nonetheless real force; society required conformity to norms of behavior, to custom, and to morality. Sometimes it did so through such formal institutions as the jury, the congregation, the church vestry, justices of the peace, and even the state legislatures. Normally, however, formal coercion was unnecessary, for every individual knew what was expected of him, and most acted accordingly. The third means of self-control, the adopting of characters, was likewise other-directed, but it was at once more positive and more selective; one searched one's soul for a character that one could play and that would win the esteem of one's peers and betters.

Now let us turn to the subject I announced at the outset, namely, the way America worked in the past in comparison with the way it works today. More specifically, let us consider how the institutions, the ideas, and the values of the Founders have held up against the barrage of changes and ideas which have besieged America and the Western world in these two hundred years.

I shall mention only in passing the constitutional order that the Framers bequeathed to us, inasmuch as, for the most part, that order has long been defunct. Government has metastasized, multiplying itself crazily and destroying its capacity to do what the Framers thought government ought to do. But we do continue to be a free people, largely because the institutionalized incompetence of Congress ensures that we get only a fraction as much government as we pay for.

The areas in which, at first blush, it would appear that we have obviously outstripped the world of the Founding generation are the material—the economic, scientific, and technological. I am not sure that members of the Founding generation, however, if they were to see and reflect upon our world, would share that appraisal. The sheer growth of the nation, in population from less than 4 million to more than 250 million and in territory from sea to sea and beyond, would not surprise them; they expected growth and planned for it. Other changes would impress them far more, but I believe they would regard these, after consideration, as mixed blessings.

For example, consider the miraculous increase in agricultural productivity. So skillful are American farmers that, though there are actually fewer of them than there were in 1787, they not only feed the country lavishly and produce unmarketable surpluses, they also have the capability of feeding the entire world. That enthusiast for scientific farming, George Washington, would be awed by what my neighbors in rural Alabama can do. But what would he say when he learned that amidst the plenty, large numbers of Americans go to bed hungry every night and that, worldwide, millions of human beings face death by starvation or illness due to malnutrition?

Or consider the general economic growth. During the early 1950s the United States became the first society in history that spent less than half its income on food, clothing, shelter, and transportation. Since then the gross national product has increased fifteen-fold—though the increase has been only three-fold if inflation is allowed for (suggesting that much of our economic activity is air). Still, no nation in history has been so affluent and had its affluence so widely shared: never before have so many had so much. But we also have something that 18th century Americans did not have: poverty. We have a permanent underclass that lives on the dole or by theft or both, that has no future and no capacity even to conceive of the future. The Framers could understand that, for they knew about the poverty of London and Paris. But they could not accept it, for they also knew that such an underclass was fatal to republics.

The most astounding changes, of course, would be those wrought by science and technology. Modern Americans take their gadgetry so much for granted that they find it difficult to imagine that scarcely a hundred years ago we were in the midst of a scientific and technological revolution that fundamentally, qualitatively changed the nature of human existence. Among the more important innovations that were in process of development were the reciprocating steam engine, with its transportation counterparts; the internal combustion engine; the electrical inventions, including their lighting, heating, transportation, and power applications; the telephone; the radio; the phonograph; the refrigerator; and powerful explosives. Each of these innovations was developed or first applied on a significant scale during the late nineteenth century, and each in some profound way suddenly brought man infinitely closer to mastering his environment. (Nature, in Her own good time, would strike back for the hubris that these achievements engendered.)

But let me here point out two different sets of implications of the scientific and technological revolution. One is that the nineteenth century changes, unlike the technology involved in the more recent "information revolution," increased man's capacity to make things and do things. The information revolution has multiplied manifold the speed with which bits of data can be processed and communicated, but it has resulted in a human overload. That is to say, we are bombarded by so many sights and sounds and numbers that we have lost our forebears' ability to think about things in the leisurely way that is essential to an enlarged understanding. It is common knowledge that, as a result, the general store of common knowledge has decreased, not increased.

The other set of implications is more subtle and at least as troublesome. Let me ease into it by pointing out that when George Washington went to New York to be sworn in as president in 1789, he had available essentially the same means of transportation that Julius Caesar had had when he crossed the Rubicon in 49 B.C. Moreover, to Washington and to Caesar, transportation and communication were synonymous terms. Indeed, except for the harness and printing, there had been virtually no major non-military technological changes during the eighteen hundred years between Caesar's time and Washington's. Because the world was the same place, it was relatively easy for eighteenth-century Americans to imagine and to identify with the ancients, as described in the Bible and the Roman and Greek classics, with which they were thoroughly familiar. The scientific and technological revolution dissolved that sense of connection: it cut Western man off from his roots in the ancient past.

It is scarcely coincidental that the period of that revolution witnessed radical changes in American higher education, a departure from the holistic and classical approach. Partly the change arose from the endowment of private colleges by new-rich industrialists, most of whom, like Andrew Carnegie, insisted that their namesake institutions concentrate on instruction that was relevant to contemporary American life. Reluctantly, the older and better colleges and universities bowed to the demand for relevance and modernized their curricula. Quite as important, perhaps more so, was pressure inside the academy. Scientific and technological training might have existed side-by-side with the classical humane studies, had not the humanities, in the language of the eminent humanist Howard Mumford Jones, "admitted a wooden horse within their walls. They permitted the concept of scientific specialization to invade their city,"[4] with the result that every branch of knowledge became fragmented and study of the humanities began to give way to study in the so-called "social sciences." Soon there was no need for requiring students to know ancient languages, and so French and German replaced Latin and Greek as the linguistic tools of scholarship. The tendency was exacerbated by the establishment of graduate schools on the model fashioned by Germany, which was leading the world in the development of specialized education. (Diehards with vested interests in classical education pointed out, sourly, that Western civilization had turned from the Mediterranean model to the Germanic once before. That had been in the fifth century, and had barbarized Europe for a thousand years.)

In the twentieth century we have, of course, moved steadily in the direction of attempting to apply the methods of science to everything. Indeed, modern man has almost come to believe that to think nonscientifically is not to think at all, or at least not to think intelligently. And yet if that were true it would be impossible to think intelligently about good and evil, or love, or justice, or law, or any of the many nonmaterial but nonetheless real things that are *truly* important, for none of these is susceptible to the kinds of observation, quantification, testing, measurement, and proof by repetition that are the essence of the scientific method.

What we must realize—and this is pivotal to an understanding of the differences between eighteenth- and twentieth-century modes of thought—is that science is merely one way of perceiving, organizing, and interpreting reality, a way that is appropriate in some instances and in others not. The point can be illustrated by an example from science itself. Newtonian physics, contrary to a popular belief, was not disproved or made obsolete by quantum mechanics; for what it describes, Newtonian physics is universally and eternally true, but it can no more be used to understand the world of the atom than nuclear physics can be used to describe the movement of the planets.

What makes this relevant to the stuff at hand is that thinking Americans of the Founding generation understood—what academics have forgotten—that formulaic thinking is not suitable to questions concerning the nature of man and society. "A great source of error," wrote Alexander Hamilton in a passage characteristic of his time and place, "is the judging of events by abstract calculations, which though geometrically true are false as they relate to the concerns of beings governed more by passion and prejudice than by an enlightened sense of their interests."[5] Instead of judging by "geometrically true abstract calculations," the Framers preferred to be guided by experience—by history, both broadly and personally conceived, both ancient and modern—and by a common-sense understanding of history, in Bolingbroke's words, as "philosophy teaching by example."

As an aside, I will admit that there were exceptions, that some eminent Americans were as capable of thinking in straight logical lines from questionable premises to silly conclusions as are, say, modern deconstructionists. Thus, Thomas Jefferson could order that his fields be laid out and sowed in precise geometric order, even though that meant that some were under water; and John Adams could embrace radical republicanism, and then monarchy, and then Malthusianism in kaleidoscopic order; and Benjamin Rush could postulate that Negritude was caused by leprosy and that if a cure for leprosy could be found nobody would ever again have to be a Negro. But most leading Americans, those who established our governmental institutions, thought in the patterns I have indicated, employing theory only when it accorded with common sense—in the modern signification of that term, not the eighteenth-century Scottish.

Perhaps the best way to demonstrate their wisdom, and to urge a return to it, will be to compare their view against the social engineers of their own time and then against what have been arguably the most powerful politico-intellectual movements of the twentieth century: Freudianism, Marxism, and cultural relativism.

The utopian social engineers of the eighteenth century usually took as a point of departure the speculations of John Locke. Every educated American was familiar with Locke's writings, and indeed the general tenor of his thinking was known to ordinary Americans, even to those who read only the Bible and the newspapers. Two of Locke's sets of ideas pertain to our subject. The first was his epistemology, as formulated in an *Essay*

*Concerning Human Understanding* (1690), and some *Thoughts Concerning Education* (1693). Locke held that there were no innate ideas, and argued instead that all human knowledge is a product of a) experience of the external world acquired through the senses and b) the inner world of introspection, or what he called "reflection." As for education, he insisted that teaching by rules and by rote was less effective than teaching by example, and that rewarding good behavior and disapproving its opposite was more efficacious in shaping character than was a list of dos and don'ts. Now, it may be that Plato and Jung are right, that there are important inborn ideas; but there is nothing kooky or flaky in Locke's empiricism.

But a succession of eighteenth-century Frenchmen, most notably La Mettrie, Condillac, and Helvetius, took Locke's epistemology and educational theories in an entirely utopian direction. They maintained that it was possible to expose children to the same experiences and education and thus make them, as adults, into people having identical passions, ideas, and thought processes. The notion of an infinitely malleable, and thus infinitely perfectible, mankind is encapsulated in the title of one of Julien La Mettrie's works, *L'Homme-machine*, or *Man a Machine* (1747). Of this sort of thinking Americans would have no part; nor did many of them think highly of Rousseau's weird theorizing about educating men to be natural.

The other part of Locke's thinking with which Americans were familiar was, of course, his natural rights theory and its companion contract theory of government and the right of revolution doctrine, as enunciated in his *Second Treatise of Civil Government* and incorporated in the Declaration of Independence. I have only two things to say on the matter here. One is that Locke is a good deal more subtle, less simple-minded, and less radical than he has been interpreted as being. The other is that, even so, his doctrines were subversive of stable government, and for that reason they were rapidly consigned to oblivion in

America after 1789. It is revealing, I think, that after the first American printing of the *Two Treatises of Civil Government* in 1773, there was no subsequent printing in the United States for 164 years, and the next favorable reference to his doctrines in an official document after 1789 that I know about is in the South Carolina ordinance of secession in 1860.

By contrast, the French gave the world Rousseau's Social Contract and the Declaration of the Rights of Man, which led inexorably to the Terror and the guillotine—to the surprise of almost no Americans, for they read and appreciated Edmund Burke's *Reflections on the Revolution in France* (1790), postulating that rights are found in history, not in nature.

Now let us turn to more modern "isms," beginning with that of Sigmund Freud. The psychological treatise which eighteenth-century Americans knew best and most thoroughly accepted was Adam Smith's *Theory of Moral Sentiments* (1759). I can illustrate how completely Americans absorbed Smith by pointing out that a number of scholars (Russell Kirk, for example) have become excited by the special wisdom to be read in the writings of one or another of the Founders (John Adams, for example), only to learn later that the Founder was quoting or paraphrasing Smith without attribution. If one knows how to look for them, one can find Smithisms in the writings of Hamilton, Madison, Washington, Jefferson, James Wilson, and a host of other Founders.

I cannot do justice to Smith's work here, and I urge you to read it for yourselves; but I can describe, in oversimplified terms, his model of the psyche. It consisted of three parts: the passions, reason, and what Smith called the "inner man." The inner man, though posited as being inside the psyche, functioned as if he were an outsider, an "impartial spectator" who observed one's behavior and expressed approval or disapproval. It can be thought of as what we should call the conscience, except that that was a notion alien to Smith, to the other Scottish philosophers, and to the Scots in general. Theirs was a "shame" culture that depended upon social approval or disapproval as the primary means of making individuals behave, as opposed to a "guilt" culture that depended upon an internalized sense of right and wrong.

It will be readily seen how Smith's model accorded with the description of the American understanding that I sketched earlier. A little more reflection will reveal the striking resemblance between Smith's passion, reason, and inner man and Freud's id, ego, and superego. I have no idea whether Freud's model derived in any way from Smith's, though I find it difficult to imagine that Freud never read Smith. Wherever Freud got it, he carried it far beyond the reasonable confines within which Smith contained it. One will find in Smith no infantile lusts, no Oedipus complex, no traumatic potty training, no castration complexes, and none of the other preoccupations of a man who grew up in the sexually repressed nineteenth century. What one will find is that Smith quite reasonably regarded character as being formed in late childhood and early adulthood, whereas Freud saw it as being shaped in a fancied and unexplorable infancy. And one will find in Smith the possibility of self improvement, but not of a utopian transformation through the magic of psychoanalysis. And a final point: when one reads the two comparatively—and I have read most of the writings of both—one emerges with an overpowering sense of Smith's wholesomeness and of Freud's sickness.

Before going on, I should add a mild demurrer. Some eighteenth-century Americans, while accepting Smith's ideas in general, thought him unrealistic in one particular. Smith believed that among the drives for self-gratification was a universal urge to improve one's condition. Alexander Hamilton, among others, thought this view overlooked the force of inertia in human affairs. "Experience teaches," Hamilton wrote, "that men are often so much governed by what they are accustomed to see and practice, that the simplest and most obvious improvements, in the most ordinary occupations, are adopted with hesitation, reluctance and by slow gradations." Men were apt to resist changes, Hamilton went on, no matter how advantageous, so long as "a bare support could be ensured by an adherence to ancient courses."[6]

Hamilton's understanding that social values and habits normally dictate economic activity, and not the other way around, leads us to the next modern ism on our agenda, that of Marxism. As Freud's intellectual pedigree includes at least indirectly thinkers who influenced the Framers, so too does that of Marx. The subject of political economy was a new one in the eighteenth century, though it had some precursors; and its most powerful pioneer thinkers—and the ones who most influenced Americans—were Scots, especially Sir James Steuart, David Hume, and Adam Smith.

Among the central concepts in the political economy of the Scottish Enlightenment was the idea that there were "stages of progress" through which societies naturally and inevitably evolve. Typically, these included hunting and gathering, herding, tillage, commerce, and manufacturing. Being disposed to think that occupation was the main determinant of character, the Scots believed that each stage bred progressively more refined manners and morals. When the manufacturing stage was reached, however, trouble was soon to follow, as dispossessed masses drifted from the country into the cities to face the drudgery of factory life and the insecurity of periodic unemployment.

Add to this picture a modified Hegelian dialectic and the dynamic of the class struggle, and you have a rudimentary Marxism. Marx took it a step further: through a wild leap of utopian prophecy described as scientific socialism, Marx forecast the increasing concentration of wealth and the increasing misery of the proletariat, followed by the last class struggle in which the proletariat would seize the means of production and a classless, stateless society would emerge. Now, the failure of Marxism, both as a system of interpreting history and as a blueprint for government, is one of the grossest and most obvious facts of the twentieth century.

But that is not my concern here: my concern is with what eighteenth-century Americans made of the Scottish ideas, and how this pertains to the state of the Republic today. Americans were much vexed about the long-range implications of the idea of the stages of progress, but not because they feared an ultimate showdown in the streets of great cities. Instead, they feared that sufficient growth and prosperity must lead to corruption, to a love of luxury, and to a love of vice. Once those set in, there could be no turning back; there could be no possible future but further decay.

I offer as a self-evident proposition the assertion that we have now arrived at such a state of corruption.

Intimately related to that development is the emergence of moral relativism. The Framers were by no means strangers to the notion that what one people regards as desirable and proper is not necessarily the same as what another people regards as desirable and proper. They were steeped in the works of Montesquieu, and Montesquieu, after a fashion, can be said to have invented that whole way of thinking. But they put it to their use, with their understanding that a regime must be suited to the manners and morals of a people if it is to endure. They would have been appalled, as I am appalled, at the modern idea that Western Civilization is no better than other civilizations, that the heritage of The West is not superior to as well as different from that of The East, that the Judaeo-Christian tradition is not morally superior to as well as different from that of Islam or paganism or tribalism, that one so-called life style is as good as another. Such thinking, if it can be so described, is a rationalization for being unable to measure up to the duty of living in accordance with and transmitting the higher values. It arises from a sense of guilt and self-loathing; and it is beyond my ken, at least among Americans, for the United States has less to feel guilty about than any other nation in the history of the world.

I could go on and deal with an assortment of other modern isms, but I should grow tedious and possibly giddy in the doing. Instead, I shall close by telling a little story for the benefit of those who still manage to believe that we have progressed over the passage of the last two centuries and can look forward to continued progress in the future.

In 1876 the city of Philadelphia hosted a Centennial Exposition, commemorating the nation's birth but also displaying the latest scientific and technical developments from all over the world. The greatest marvel on display was the gigantic Corliss cross-compound reciprocating steam engine, a mass of furnaces and boilers and tubes, fashioned by the hand and wit of man and having the power of five thousand horses. The historian Henry Adams, stricken with awe upon seeing the magnificent Corliss engine, was inspired to write an essay called "The Virgin and the Dynamo." For more than a millennium, he wrote, the Virgin Mary had been the symbol of frail mankind's hope for salvation in an otherwise indifferent and unfathomable universe. Now the dynamo had emerged as a symbol, not of hope but of defiant confidence in man's power.

In another quarter of the city, several visiting Frenchmen, their imaginations equally fired by the marvels they had seen, were discussing them and speculating as to what further miracles man might perform.

"Some day," one of them said, "science will develop a small, self-contained engine that will be able to propel vehicles at high speeds without being affixed to tracks."

"Pah!" said another. "Not only that. Men will be able to attach wings to such a vehicle and fly."

"You have no imagination," countered a third. "In due course men will be able to fly away from the earth entirely and explore the heavens."

And so it went, somebody prophesying the sending of sounds and even pictures through the ether, another suggesting that man would become able to control the weather—each forecast more fabulous than the last.

Finally, inevitably, someone said, "But all that is as nothing, my friends. Someday, someday, man will be able to conquer death itself."

There was a stunned silence, and then an onlooker, who had said nothing earlier, spoke up. "Perhaps. And just at that time, God, sporting a long grey beard and wearing a flowing white robe, will jangle his chain of keys and announce, 'Closing time, gentlemen.'"

## ENDNOTES

1. Phillips Payson, "A Sermon," Boston, 1778, in Charles S. Hyneman and Donald S. Lutz, eds., *American Political Writing during the Founding Era, 1760-1805* (2 vols., Indianapolis, 1983), 1:529.

2. Quoted in Philip Greven, *The Protestant Temperament: Patterns of Child-Rearing, Religious Experience, and the Self in Early America* (New York, 1977), 346.

3. Thomas Jefferson to the Inhabitants of Albemarle County, April 3, 1809, in H.A. Washington, ed., *The Writings of Thomas Jefferson* (17 vols., New York, 1854), 5:349, and Jefferson to Dupont de Nemours, March 2, 1809, in Merrill Peterson, comp., *Thomas Jefferson: Writings* (New York, 1984), 1203.

4. Howard Mumford Jones, "The Place of the Humanities in American Education," in Sharon Brown, ed., *Present Tense* (New York, 1946), 80.

5. Alexander Hamilton to _____, December 1779-March 1780, in Harold S. Syrett, ed., *The Papers of Alexander Hamilton* (26 vols., New York, 1961-79), 2:242.

6. Alexander Hamilton, "Report on the Subject of Manufactures," December 5, 1791, in Syrett, ed., *Papers of Hamilton*, 10:266-67.

# The Demise of Federalism:
## With Consent of the Governed?

ROBERT T. DONNELLY

In America, we have had two written forms of national government since the end of the Revolutionary War.

The first was the Articles of Confederation, a written constitution which failed primarily because Congress was not given the power to tax and to regulate commerce among the states.

The second was the written Constitution of 1787. By its terms it established a strong national government. Because of a belief that it was not sufficiently explicit as to rights of individuals and the states, the ten original amendments were adopted in 1791.

The prevailing view in 1791 was that the national government had only delegated powers, that the states had an undefined range of powers and that reserved to the people was an undefined *sphere of non-government* within which people may not be interfered with by government.

This concept was articulated formally in the Tenth Amendment to the United States Constitution: "The powers not delegated to the United States by the constitution, nor prohibited by it to the states, are reserved to the states respectively, or to the people."[1]

Fifty years ago, the Tenth Amendment was considered impregnable. Today the Tenth Amendment may be obsolete. How could this have happened in America? In my view, any discussion of its demise must be prefaced by noting three dates:

(1) On May 31, 1913, the Seventeenth Amendment, which

provides for the direct election of United States Senators, was declared ratified;

(2) On September 29, 1958, the United States Supreme Court declared that its decisions are the Supreme Law of the Land under Article VI of the Constitution;

(3) On February 19, 1985, the United States Supreme Court virtually excised the Tenth Amendment from the Constitution.

(1)

Prior to ratification of the Seventeenth Amendment, United States Senators were chosen by the legislatures of the states.[2] Within the structures of the original Constitution was the assurance that the United States Senate would be directly and politically accountable to the states. "The House of Representatives will derive its powers from the people of America . . . . So far the government is *national*, not *federal*. The Senate, on the other hand, will derive its powers from the States as political and coequal societies . . . . So far the government is *federal*, not *national* . . . . From this aspect of the government it appears to be of a mixed character, presenting at least as many *federal* as *national* features."[3] We know now that any assurance of political accountability to the states as political entities was obliterated by the Seventeenth Amendment.

(2)

In *Brown v. Board of Education*,[4] the Supreme Court of the United States outlawed racial segregation in the public schools of the states.

On September 29, 1958, in *Cooper v. Aaron*,[5] against a backdrop of overwhelming acceptance of *Brown*, the United States Supreme Court asserted for the first time in its history and in the history of the nation that *its interpretations* of the written Constitution *in a particular case in one State* constitute the "supreme law of the land" under Article VI of the Constitution and are of binding effect in *all of the States*. In *Cooper*, the Court asserted:

> Article VI of the Constitution makes the Constitution the "supreme Law of the Land." In 1803, Chief Justice Marshall, speaking for a unanimous Court, referring to the Constitution as "the fundamental and paramount law of the nation," declared in the notable case of *Marbury v. Madison*, 1 Cranch 137, 177, that "It is emphatically the province and duty of the judicial department to say what the law is." This decision declared the basic principle that the federal judiciary is supreme in the exposition of the law of the Constitution, and that principle has ever since been respected by this Court and the country as a permanent and indispensable feature of our constitutional system. It follows that *the interpretation* of the Fourteenth Amendment *enunciated by this Court* in the *Brown* case is the *supreme law of the land*, and Art. VI of the Constitution makes it of binding effect on the States "any Thing in the Constitution or Laws of any State to the Contrary notwithstanding" (emphasis added).[6]

In *Cooper*, the Court enabled itself to "work out principles of legality, equality, and the rest, revise these principles from time to time in the light of what seems to the Court fresh moral insight, and judge the acts of . . . the states . . . accordingly."[7]

The opinion in *Brown* drew its "inspiration from consecrated principles."[8] It has already secured its place in history by virtue of its declaration for decency and justice. But it is a fact that as a result of *Cooper* and its progeny, the direction of social policy in America is, in enormous measure, now set by persons not accountable to the people. They have adroitly implanted the notion that it should be the role of the United States Supreme Court "to articulate the moral sense of abstract principles of just government in contemporary circumstances."[9]

*By way of example*: In *Roe v. Wade*,[10] in the exercise of power it gave itself in *Cooper*, the Supreme Court abrogated abortion statutes in *all* of the States. In *Bigelow v. Virginia*,[11] in an attempt to buttress the *Roe* decision, the Court held that the right to advertise a New York abortion clinic in Virginia is protected by the First Amendment and transformed First Amendment free speech from Holmes' "marketplace of ideas" concept to protection of business advertising. The result was *Bates v. State Bar*,[12] in which the Court invalidated state limitations on lawyer advertising and changed the practice of law from a profession to a business.

(3)

On February 19, 1985, in *Garcia v. San Antonio Metropolitan Transit Authority*,[13] the question was whether the Commerce Clause empowers Congress to enforce the requirements of the Fair Labor Standards Act against the States "in areas of traditional governmental functions."[14]

The majority rejected the "traditional function" model because it "*inevitably invites an unelected federal judiciary to make decisions about which state policies it favors and which ones it dislikes*" (emphasis added).[15]

It then turned its back on its duty of judicial review under the Tenth Amendment and used as rationale an assumption that the "*political process* ensures that laws that unduly burden the States will not be promulgated" (emphasis added).[16]

It is difficult to discuss the *Garcia* opinion objectively. At least since *Shapiro v. Thompson*,[17] the justices of the Supreme Court have routinely substituted their views on social policy for statutes enacted by state legislatures. And, given the impact of political action committee money spent in senatorial contests in the interest of national agenda, the majority opinion in *Garcia* must be characterized as a retreat from political reality.

In the view of Justice Powell, the majority in *Garcia* rejected "almost 200 years of the understanding of the constitutional status of federalism."[18] It took the "unprecedented view that Congress is free under the Commerce Clause to assume a state's traditional sovereign power, and to do so without judicial review of its action."[19] Of course, there is precedent for the Powell view:

> The courts enforce the legislative will when ascertained, if within the constitutional grant of power. Within its legitimate sphere, Congress is supreme, and beyond the control of the courts; but if it steps outside of its constitutional limitations, and attempts that which is beyond its reach, the courts are authorized to, and when called upon in due course of legal proceedings must, annul its encroachments upon the reserved power of the States and the people.[20]

It must be said that the Court's reluctance to perpetuate "unworkable" distinctions between state and federal "functions" in *Garcia* stands as abdication. That an analytical framework is cumbersome affords little excuse to imbalance the governmental branches through blind faith in "the effectiveness of the federal political process in preserving the State's interests . . . ."[21] In marked contrast is the Court's taste for activism in the Fourteenth Amendment arena. These inconsistent jurisprudential postures work an inversion of respective constitutional powers and responsibilities not intended by the Framers of the original Constitution and the Fourteenth Amendment.

The Fourteenth Amendment, in relevant part, provides:

> Section 1. . . . No State shall make or enforce any law which shall abridge the privileges or immunities of citizens of the United States; nor shall any State deprive any person of life, liberty, or property, without due process of law; nor deny to any person within its jurisdiction the equal protection of the laws.

Section 5. The Congress shall have power to enforce by appropriate legislation, the provisions of this article.

In *Ex parte Virginia*,[22] decided when the history of the Amendment was fresh in the recollection of the justices, the Court stated that the Thirteenth and Fourteenth Amendments "were intended to be, what they really are, limitations of the power of the States and enlargements of the *power of Congress*" (emphasis added).[23]

The Court then referred to Section 5, the "enforcement section" of the Fourteenth Amendment, and said:

All of the amendments derive much of their force from this latter provision. It is not said the *judicial power* of the general government shall extend to enforcing the prohibitions and to protecting the rights and immunities guaranteed. It is not said that branch of the government shall be authorized to declare void any action of a State in violation of the prohibitions. It is the power of Congress which has been enlarged. Congress is authorized to *enforce* the prohibitions by appropriate legislation. Some legislation is contemplated to make the amendments fully effective. Whatever legislation is appropriate, that is, adapted to carry out the objects the amendments have in view, whatever tends to enforce submission to the prohibitions they contain, and to secure to all persons the enjoyment of perfect equality of civil rights and the equal protection of the laws against state denial or invasion, if not prohibited, is brought within the domain of congressional power.[24]

The teaching of *Ex parte Virginia*, written twelve years after the Fourteenth Amendment was declared ratified, was that

Congress, not the Court, should implement the provisions of the Fourteenth Amendment and that determinations made by Congress should prevail "if not prohibited" by the Tenth Amendment.

If, as some believe, the original written Constitution was intended to implant a structure which would assure *integrity of process*, it was arguable, before *Garcia*, that the Framers contemplated a system of judicial review under Article III, Section 2 by which the Court would confine Congress to the powers given it by Article I, Section 8 and would apply the proscriptions of the first ten amendments.

If, as some believe, Section 5 of the Fourteenth Amendment was intended to empower Congress to enforce its provisions against the states, it was also arguable, before *Garcia*, that a system of judicial review was contemplated by which the Court would apply the proscriptions of the Tenth Amendment against action taken by Congress under its Section 5 mandate.

Integrity of process is the base on which our constitutional system of government is built. "The impartial and consistent administration of laws and institutions, whatever their substantive principles, we may call formal justice . . . . Formal justice is adherence to principle, or as some have said, obedience to system . . . . Formal justice in the case of legal institutions is simply an aspect of the rule of law which supports and secures legitimate expectations."[25]

Alexander Bickel referred to this concept as "the morality of process" and described its fall from grace as follows:

> The assault upon the legal order by moral imperatives was not only or perhaps even most effectively an assault from the outside. As I have suggested, it came as well from within, in the Supreme Court headed for fifteen years by Earl Warren. When a lawyer stood before him arguing his side of a case on the basis of some legal doctrine or other, or making a procedural

point, or contending that the Constitution allocated competence over a given issue to another branch of government than the Supreme Court or to the states rather than to the federal government, the chief justice would shake him off saying, "Yes, yes, yes, but is it [whatever the case exemplified about law or about the society], is it right? Is it good?" More than once, and in some of its most important actions, the Warren Court got over doctrinal difficulties or issues of the allocation of competences among various institutions by asking what it viewed as a decisive practical question: If the Court did not take a certain action which was *right* or *good*, would other institutions do so, given political realities? The Warren Court took the greatest pride in cutting through legal technicalities, in piercing through procedure to substance. But legal technicalities are the stuff of law, and piercing through a particular substance to get to procedures suitable to many substances is in fact what the task of law most often is.[26]

It would border on the ridiculous to suggest that the clock can be turned back now. And what the Court has done was, for the most part, *right* and *good*. But what if the result of future deviation from process is *wrong* and *bad*? Where will the appeal lie?

In *Katzenbach v. Morgan*,[27] the Court recognized that Section 5 of the Fourteenth Amendment "is a positive grant of legislative power authorizing Congress to exercise its discretion in determining whether and what legislation is needed to secure the guarantees of the Fourteenth Amendment."[28] The Court refused to recognize a right in Congress to dilute equal protection and due process decisions of the Court.[29] And it considered whether the legislation enacted by Congress was appropriate "to enforce the Equal Protection Clause . . . ."[30]

The teaching of *Katzenbach* and *Garcia* is that a model outside the Constitution is nearing completion: (1) Under the *Cooper* assertion and the Incorporation Doctrine the Court will sit as a Council of Revision over the states;[31] (2) the Court will no longer defend the states against action taken by Congress under the aegis of the Commerce Clause; and (3) if Congress should undertake to address the parameters of the Fourteenth Amendment, the Court will decide if its articulations are *right* and *good*. Of course, (1) and (2) are in place. Only time can tell as to (3). Recent history would indicate that the preference of Congress is to second-guess policy rather than make it.

In sum, the notion of federalism is no more than a legal fiction today. Any *political* incentive for the National Government to respect states' interests was obliterated by the Seventeenth Amendment. Any *legal* incentive has been abandoned by the Supreme Court. Instead of protecting the legitimate interests of the states, the Supreme Court competes with Congress to dictate to the states their "legitimate" interests.

The drafters of the Fourteenth Amendment recognized and articulated instances in which the states' interests must yield. They provided that Congress determine the mechanism by which to compromise these interests, subject to Supreme Court review under the Tenth Amendment. Yet today, with less at stake in states' interests and little, if any, homage paid to the Tenth Amendment, Congress rarely acts to enforce the Fourteenth Amendment and the Supreme Court has taken to itself the power to enforce its provisions with decisions of the Court, which now stand as the "supreme law of the land" under the *Cooper* assertion.

Being somewhat old-fashioned, elimination of federalism from the Constitution *without involving the people* makes me uneasy. I sense that circumvention of the constitutional amendment process makes The Rule of Law vulnerable. Elitists will dismiss this expression of concern as "a quixotic tilt at windmills which belittles great principles of liberty."[32] But the essence of the relationship between the people and their government is that the people, not the Court, are sovereign. The people, not the Court, should "articulate the moral sense of abstract principles of just government in contemporary circumstances."[33]

## ENDNOTES

1. Constitution of the United States of America, Amendment X.

2. U.S. Constitution, Article I, Section 3.

3. *Federalist* No. 39. Madison, in *The Federalist*, John C. Hamilton, ed. (Philadelphia: J.B. Lippincott & Co., 1873).

4. 347 U.S. 483 (1954).

5. *Cooper v. Aaron*, 358 U.S. 1 (1958).

6. *Ibid.* at 18.

7. Ronald Dworkin, *Taking Rights Seriously.* (Cambridge: Harvard University Press, 1977). p. 137.

8. Benjamin N. Cardozo, *The Nature of the Judicial Process.* (New Haven: Yale University Press, 1921).

9. Richards. *Constitutional Interpretation, History, and the Death Penalty: A Book Review.* 71 Calif.L.Rev. 1372, 1397 (1983).

10. 410 U.S. 113 (1973).

11. 421 U.S. 809 (1975).

12. 433 U.S. 350 (1977).

13. 469 U.S. 528 (1985).

14. *Ibid.*, at 530.

15. *Ibid.*, at 546.

16. *Ibid.*, at 556.

17. 394 U.S. 618 (1969).

18. 469 U.S., at 560 (Powell, J., dissenting).

19. *Ibid.*, at 575.

20. *United States v. Reese*, 92 U.S. 214, 221 (1875); see also *McCulloch v. Maryland.*, 17 U.S. (4 Wheaton) 316, 415 (1819).

21. *Garcia*, 469 U.S. at 552.

22. 100 U.S. 339 (1880).

23. *Ibid.*, at 345.

24. *Ibid.*, at 345-346.

25. J. Rawls, *A Theory of Justice.* (Cambridge: Belknap Press of Harvard University

Press, 1971). p. 58, 59.

26. Alexander Bickel, *The Morality of Consent*. (New Haven: Yale University Press, 1975). pp. 120-121.

27. 384 U.S. 641 (1966).

28. *Ibid.*, at 651.

29. See Cox. *The Role of Congress in Constitutional Determination*, 40 U. Cinn L. Rev. 199. (1971).

30. 384 U.S. at 651.

31. See: Raoul Berger, *Government by Judiciary*. (Cambridge: Harvard University Press, 1977). pp. 300-306.

32. *Kunz v. New York*, 340 U .S. 290, 295 (1950) (Jackson, J., dissenting).

33. Richards, *op. cit.* 1397.

# The Constitution, Not Just a Law: A Dissent from Misspelled Original Intent[1]

### W. B. ALLEN

Philadelphian Benjamin Rush had cause to worry early in 1787, and he shared his worries with his countrymen. Writing appropriately enough in a new journal entitled *The American Museum*, Rush speculated whether his country might become a relic before consummating the promise of its Revolution. The war ended long before the Revolution, for the Revolution had no end but "to establish and perfect our new forms of government, and to prepare the principles, morals, and manners of our citizens, for these forms of government. . . ."[2] When Rush emphasized at the end of his essay, "The Revolution is not over!" he meant then that the specific intent or design of the Revolution remained to be accomplished.

That perspective or attitude toward the Founding was not unique to Rush. It characterized the Founding, and many of the Founders, in general. Because of that original attitude, Americans since have confronted a special difficulty—namely, how to acquire or preserve a metric whereby to test fidelity to the purpose the Founders believed to have realized. That question poses a special difficulty because it entails a logical corollary—namely, whether the Constitution itself is adequate? Or, should a revolution begin?

The question of revolution—the contemporary prospect of a rebellion against the present forms and prospects of American life is easily the most interesting and important question in the entire original intent debate. Without positing such a limiting condition, that debate declines to sterile exercises in legal reasoning. Accordingly, I ask that we face squarely up to the question of revolution, as George Washington did in the midst of the Stamp Act crisis when he wrote, "Law can never make just what is in its nature unjust."[3] This moral declaration of independence will always be the philosophical pre-condition of a political declaration of independence.[4]

The *possibility* of such a moral declaration undergirds the original intent debate. The original intent researcher poses less a question about the clarity with which the past speaks to the present than a question about the acceptable grounds of obedience—of legitimate authority—in the present. To raise the question is to threaten to withdraw consent (or submission, if the stolid persist), to de-legitimize established authority. From that step there remains only one progressive direction: revolution.

We cannot contemplate such a possibility in ignorance. We require to master both the objective conditions which counsel rebellion and the principles which enable us to discern its necessity. In what follows I seek to develop these two qualifications of rebellion, starting from the terms of the present debate itself. I announced in the title of this essay that "original intent" has been pervasively misspelled. When we discern the correct spelling, then we can analyze its political and legal significance.

Lawyers are wont to express technical concepts in Latin. In the original intent debate, they have used the word "original" as though they derived it from *ab initio*, from the beginning. In that sense, "original intent" has no greater significance than attaches to what comes first in a series. As such, it has neither dignity nor compulsive meaning. True, the human praise of the venerable is one of the more charming virtues. It is, however, far from sufficient, inasmuch as the old commands our attention only for so long as it is allied to an argument for goodness. Naboth yielded his life in defense of ancestors he regarded as better than himself, not contemptible forebears. What comes first is older but not, for that reason, better. Thus, the *intentio ab initio* cannot command our respect, and no one with respect for our intelligence can offer it to us as doing so. That spelling of original intent is incorrect.

An alternative source for the meaning of "original" is *a principio*, a word which can mean not only "from the beginning" but more importantly "from a principle." It stands thus as a claim, significant not because of its authors but because of its demands on us (*en arche ein ho logos*). Original intent thus emphasizes the intention or design as it applies to us and as we, in principle, are capable of understanding it. It possesses a dignity in proportion as it truly reflects that rational design which operates compulsively on minds unaffected by desire. When it is old its dignity is enhanced by virtue of its having survived challenges to its status as a superior claim. The only original intent worthy of the name is such a one, become manifest in the form of responding fully to our most serious questions even after we have pursued counter hypotheses.

Investigating the debate with some care, we will see that the misspelled variety of original intent has characteristically been propounded. We will also readily perceive that that version poses little threat to the legal and political order as it subsists today, while the correct version would deliver us to the very threshold of revolution.

More than a slight hint of this can be found in one of the most recent contributions to this debate, by Raoul Berger. The very title of his long essay conveys this ambiguous relationship: *Federalism: The Founders' Design.*[5] He used the word "design," rather than the word "intent," as much a term of art as of moral purpose. Design may mean aim or intention, but it may also point to the inherent *logos* or principle in accord with which a work was executed. A given work may aim to do good without being adequately designed to hit the mark. If the Founders aimed at federalism, or liberty, or anything else, but did not adequately tailor their efforts to their purpose, it would require an argument passing bizarre to persuade men to adhere to such foredoomed efforts.

Within the essay, Berger recurs far less to the term "design" than to "original intent," doubtless because that it is how the debate has already been cast. Which original intent is prominent, the *ab initio* or the *a principio*? The virtue of Berger's analysis is that he demonstrates that the concept of "original intent" is not a term of art. It has characterized American jurisprudence from the beginning and before; indeed, Berger shows the term to be a staple of legislative interpretation in the Anglo-American universe from as much as 500 years before the Founding. When we canvas Berger's sources, we are of two minds about the spelling question, some sources alighting on one side and others on the other side of the question.

The confusion derives from the fact that the concept of original intent has been promiscuously applied to statutes and constitutions as though it made little difference to which one referred. Thus, "such construction ought to be put upon a statute, as may best answer the intention which the makers of it had in view."[6] Berger cited this formulation as the proper gloss on his own statement to the effect that, to understand correctly what is "nowhere mentioned in the Constitution, we must look to the explanations of the Founders, what is characterized as the 'original intention.'" Berger also cited James Madison's famous gloss: "the *sense* in which the Constitution was accepted and ratified" must guide every expounding. Madison's expanded version of his argument, however, permits us to question whether his view says no more than that "'the intention of the lawmaker is the law,' rising even above the text."[7] Madison located

> a key *sense* of the Constitution, where alone the true one can be found; in the proceedings of the Convention, the contemporary expositions, and above all in

the ratifying conventions of the States. If the *instru-ment* be interpreted by criticisms which lose sight of the *intentions of the parties to it*, in the fascinating pursuit of objects of public advantage or convenience, the purest motives can be no security against innova-tion materially changing the features of the Govern-ment.[8]

The law, as the command of a sovereign, stands in relation to an individual differently than an *instrument* of social compact, an agreement, to which one may be party. For even where the agreement exists as historical antecedent to a contemporary claim of sovereignty, the "intentions of the parties to it" cannot reveal a *sense* in the same way that a sovereign command can reveal an intention or mind. A sovereign mind, individual or corporate, may be seized by the purpose it aims at—the sovereign mind by definition singular of purpose. An agreement, however, offers plural minds by definition, and the very idea of agreement constrains the identification of the intention to what each of several will specifically ratify—always somewhat less than what each would himself declare. In agreement, then, it is far less the several reasons for agreeing than the agreement itself which expresses intent, while in the case of law, it is the purpose even more than the literal text ("rising above the text," Berger said) which expresses intent. This difference is of the greatest conse-quence.

Now let us contrast Berger's authority with that of Cooley. The model for Berger:

> Thus, light was first to be sought from the makers' "declaration of their myndes," and in the absence of such a declaration, from those that, "were moste neerest the statute."[9]

A rule in literary exegesis is to discover authorial intent. A like rule can apply to statutes, for a legislature acts on authority, whether assumed or derived, which permits the authorial stance. The "informal propositions" of a constitutional convention are surely authored but possess no authority. Thus, Cooley commented:

> Every member of [a constitutional] convention acts upon such motives and reasons as influence him personally, and the motions and debates do not necessarily indicate the purpose of a majority of a convention in adopting a particular clause . . . . And even if it were certain we had attained to the meaning of the convention, it is by no means to be allowed a controlling force, especially if that meaning appears not to be the one which the words would most naturally and obviously convey. For as the Constitution does not derive its force from the Convention which framed, but from the people who ratified it, the intent to be arrived at is that of the people, and it is not to be supposed that they have looked for any dark or abstruse meaning in the words employed, but rather that they have accepted them in the sense most obvious to the common understanding . . . . These proceedings therefore are less conclusive of the proper construction of the instrument than are legislative proceedings of the proper construction of a statute; since in the latter case it is the intent of the legislature we seek, while in the former we are endeavoring to arrive at the intent of the people through the discussions and deliberations of their representatives.[10]

There is, then, a tension between legislative original intent and constitutional original intent, to which Berger pays only implicit attention in his book. In pointing this out and, ultimately, dissenting from Berger's view, I intend to narrow or tighten rather than to overthrow his conception. To do justice to his argument, however, I need first to draw it out in a length appropriate to the effort he expended on it.

The object of Berger's vigorous opposition is that view of constitutionalism which liberates the present from all historical strictures, a view variously known as "non-interpretivism," the "unwritten constitution," the "evolutionary constitution," and other familiar terms of art. In one such instance, he reasons as follows:

> Does long-standing adherence of the Courts to an unconstitutional course, allegedly "acquiesced" in by Congress and the people, sanction it? Gerald Lynch would extenuate departures from the text as well as from the original understanding on grounds of "adherence to long-standing constitutional doctrines," and he asserts that "the people have implicitly ratified the role the Court has assumed over the last century."[11]

It would only be fair to point out that Lynch would not apply Berger's term, "unconstitutional," to this process. He would rather describe it as the specific form of constitutional existence. Nevertheless, Berger's point is clear—tacit acceptance of non-consecrated doctrines does not qualify as a principle of legitimation (or a rational justification of submission to authority or power). In accord with that argument, the litmus of legitimacy must be an explicit original text of understanding. A different response than Berger's might have invoked the language of the Declaration of Independence and judged Lynch's long-standing departures as a "long train of abuses" patiently suffered while sufferable on the prudential ground that native reaction should not proceed from "light and transient" reasons. That approach would have led Berger toward a different view of original intent than that he envisions. Instead, he settled for the version contained in Leonard Levy's response:

> The simple fact is that at no time in our history have

the American people passed judgment, pro or con, on the merits of judicial review over Congress. Consent freely given, by referendum, by legislation, or amendment, is simply not the same as failure to abolish or impair.[12]

Now, Levy's view is such that the expression or absence of expression of consent operates not so much as a principle than as a positive enactment. And positive enactment, with understanding behind it, is what Berger seeks in original intent. The intention is rather the *product* (including the understanding) than the *moral purposes* of such a singular, historical event. For that reason Berger re-affirmed the frequently stated Court position, one defended by James Madison, that "a contemporaneous legislative exposition of the Constitution when the Founders . . . were actively participating in public affairs, long acquiesced in, fixes the construction . . . ."[13] This is some distance removed from Justice Harry Blackmun's preferred view, that "the text of the Constitution provides the beginning rather than the final answer to every inquiry into questions of federalism."[14]

One sees in this formulation the difference between Lynch's "long-standing adherence" and the "long acquiescence" of *Hampton and Co. v. United States*.[15] Reliance on authority derived purely from positive tradition characterizes each view, and they are distinguished only by differing notions of the source of the tradition. The Lynch view will settle upon the first available historical source, counting backwards (thus, too, Mr. Justice Brennan), while Berger and the Court have insisted upon a single, unique tradition. No compelling moral argument is made for either, doubtless because each approach confuses a rule of prudence (tradition is a powerful aid to memory and judgment) with a rule of interpretation (to follow tradition exclusively depends upon its being superior to every other possible recourse).

Berger's purpose is praiseworthy. He sought a rule whereby to safeguard society from what Madison called "a will independent of society." Seeking to check the power of the Court, he naturally looked to the Founding, and there he sought a constraint which would not depend on the will of the party to be constrained. As he put it, "Those who enjoy the exercise of uncurbed power are unlikely to surrender it merely because it has been usurped." Justice White similarly, in the 1986 sodomy case, pointed out that "the Court . . . comes nearest to illegitimacy when it deals with judge-made constitutional law having little or no cognizable roots in the language or design of the Constitution."[16] The problem for White and Berger alike, however, is that they have fashioned a device to limit judicial usurpation, misspelled original intent, which calls upon the justices themselves for its execution. Original intent is neither self-executing nor falls to any of the other branches of government to execute. The power of the Court, reposing as it does on Justice John Jay's 1793 ruling on advisory opinions, which insisted that the Court must have the last word, cannot be directly constrained by any ordinary institutional considerations.[17] This seems to have been the import of the argument in Marshall's original elaboration of the notion of judicial review, in which most commentators usually neglect that the Chief Justice also laid out the limits of the power.

> By the Constitution of the United States, the President is invested with certain important political powers, in the exercise of which he is to use his own discretion, and is accountable only to his country in his political character . . . . The subjects are political. They respect the nation's, not individual rights, and . . . the decision of the executive is conclusive . . . where the heads of departments are the political or confidential agents of the executive . . . to act in cases in which the executive possesses a constitutional or legal discretion, nothing can be more clear than that their acts are only

politically examinable.[18]

Marshall's account of judicial review describes it as law-bound, subject to the Constitution and not as a carte blanche constitutional oversight. The reason is that the Constitution provides not only for legislative but for political judgment. In that context, he held, the "province of the Court is, solely, to decide on the rights of individuals," which is not to say "minorities."[19] Thus, when it came to the question of original intent Marshall could affirm a rather different view than prevails today:

> That the people have an original right to establish for their future government, such principles as in their opinion, shall most conduce to their happiness, is the basis on which the whole American fabric has been erected . . . as the authority from which [the principles] proceed is supreme, and can seldom act, they are designed to be permanent.[20]

Original "original intent," in other words, focussed not on the absence of referenda but on the *presence* of the original authoritative act. Thus, Justice Joseph Story could maintain that the Court could construe only the powers of the Constitution and not "the policy or principles which induced the grant of them," precisely because "the Constitution has proceeded upon a theory of its own."[21] Contemporary jurists have been known to echo similar sentiments, though seldom to stick by them. Justice Powell, for example, and whom we shall see explicitly rejecting the restraint on the judicial creation of rights, nevertheless held in 1973 that "it is not the province of this Court to create substantive constitutional rights."[22] The late Justice Harlan, on the other hand, sounded in 1970 much like his original namesake:

> When the Court disregards the express intent and understanding of the Framers, it has invaded the realm of the political process, . . . and it has violated the

constitutional structure which it is its highest duty to protect.[23]

Contrasting with Harlan, however, is the dissenting opinion of Justice Brennan, which more nearly approximates the professional consensus on the question of original intent in the contemporary world:

> [The] historical record left by the framers of the 14th Amendment, because it is a product of differing and conflicting political pressures and conceptions of federalism, is thus too vague and imprecise to provide us with sure guidance in deciding . . . . We must therefore conclude that its framers understood their Amendment to be a broadly worded injunction capable of being interpreted by future generations in accordance with the vision and needs of those generations.[24]

On such terms as these, original intent would refer to the structures of government and the original authority of the people last of all!

To repeat: misspelled original intent does not constrain the Court beyond the willingness of justices to operate within what is essentially the framework of a hypothetical construct. To realize the goal of Berger's crusade, Americans would have to rediscover a means to limit the Court not dependent on the opinions of the justices. Before we assess the prospects of accomplishing this, let me restate the cause of the central error in the prevailing reading of original intent.

Original intent has been confused with the doctrine of legislative intention. Brennan errs thus in the citation from *Oregon v. Mitchell* above, but both sides are guilty of this. Even the reference to Justice Taney's discussion in the *Dred Scott* case as the *locus classicus* for the meaning of original intent results from confusion.[25] Taney employed the model of legislative intention to build his argument of the "intent of the framers" regarding black people. He searched the references and practices common to the Framers as a means to discern their intention in the substantive provisions of their enactments. The process mirrors the rummaging of the "legislative record" which characterizes contemporary Court proceedings. We saw an example of this in 1987, when the Supreme Court decided that Jews and Arabs qualify as ethnic minorities on the strength of remarks made during the deliberations of the Reconstruction Congress.[26]

By contrast, the correct understanding of original intent would not pretend to lift substantive decisions on particular facts whole from some founding record. Unlike legislative intention, which *may* guide the Court, original intent operates to constrain the entire American political system with respect to processes and ends. The substance of the principle is republicanism—self-government.

The consequence of taking this distinction seriously will be to undermine the prevailing understanding of this particular question, one that has been much on the minds of many people in recent years and part of an academic debate in the legal community stretching back at least thirty years. In discussing the interpretation of the Constitution, we are forced to choose whether we wish to discuss the specific and limited role assigned to the Court or the broader question of the structure and operation of the American political system. A palpable example of the effect such a distinction would have on the Court was offered in the majority opinion in *INS v. Chadha*.[27] By insisting on a rigorous interpretation of the separation of powers, focussing on the presentment clauses, the Court found itself unable to reach the policy question (despite the vigorous objection of Justice White). More importantly, however, in a rare twentieth-century instance the Court acknowledged dimensions of governmental power beyond its reach. In *Chadha*, form outweighed substance, meaning therefore that substantive decisions remained to be made in forums and in a manner beyond the power of the Court to impose. Not utility, but constitutional design decided the question, and in constitutional matters original intent can mean nothing less. To maintain his point, the Chief Justice summoned James Madison to his defense, but not Madison's most explicit statement on the question:

> I am not unaware that my belief, not to say knowledge, of the views of those who proposed the Constitution, and what is of more importance, my deep impression as to the views of those who bestowed on it the stamp of authority, may influence my interpretation of the Instrument. On the other hand, it is not impossible that those who consult the instrument without a danger of that bias, may be exposed to an equal one in their anxiety to find in its text an authority for a particular measure of great apparent utility.[28]

> Serious danger seems to be threatened to the genuine sense of the Constitution, not only by an unwarrantable latitude of construction, but by the use made of precedents which cannot be supposed to have had in the view of their Authors the bearing contended for, and even where they may have crept through inadvertence into acts of Congress, and been signed by the Executive at a midnight hour, in the midst of a group scarcely admitting perusal, and under a wariness of mind as little admitting a vigilant attention.
>
> Another, and perhaps a greater danger, is to be apprehended from the influence which the usefulness and popularity of measures may have on questions of their constitutionality.[29]

In Madison's view, as in the *Chadha* opinion, then, the key to constitutional jurisprudence is a careful segregation of legislative intent and constitutional intent, the former bowing to the latter even where utility pleads its case.

The Court is able to apply this rule only in the circumstance where it preserves its own power in a properly subordinated role. In that sense, the defenders of misspelled original intent have inverted the argument, for they behold a Court which is able to hold the government's feet to the fire of constitutional structure not by virtue of its own subordinate role but rather by virtue of its superordinate judgment.

The clearest example of this inversion appears in the writings of Judge Robert Bork, who reasons that it is sufficient for jurists to begin with a "premise" rooted in the Constitution in order to fulfill the function of preserving constitutional intention. Judge Bork sets forth the peculiar problem which confronts the Court in unmistakable terms, terms which convey far more than the limited, subordinate role envisioned in this essay. I quote at length:

> The problem for constitutional law always has been and always will be the resolution of what has been called the Madisonian dilemma. The United States was founded as what we now call a Madisonian system, one which allows majorities to rule in wide areas of life simply because they are majorities, but which also holds that individuals have some freedoms that must be exempt from majority control. The dilemma is that neither the majority nor the minority can be trusted to define the proper spheres of democratic authority and individual liberty. The first would court tyranny by the majority; the second tyranny by the minority.
>
> Over time it came to be thought that the resolution of the Madisonian problem—the definition of majority power and minority freedom—was primarily the function of the judiciary and, most especially, the function of the Supreme Court. That understanding, which

now seems a permanent feature of our political arrangements, creates the need for constitutional theory. The courts must be energetic to protect the rights of individuals but they must also be scrupulous not to deny the majority's legitimate right to govern. How can that be done?[30]

Before entertaining Judge Bork's response to this most important question, we must note how far his account of the Madisonian problem and system depart from what was in fact the case.

Judge Bork attributes to the United States Constitution characteristics which Madison specifically attributed only to systems not vested with the safeguards of the Constitution. *Federalist* Number Ten spells out at great length the difference between mere majority rule (simple democracy) and the extended republic (representative democracy). Majorities not only are *not* allowed to rule in the latter "simply because they are majorities," but only just majorities are allowed to rule.[31] Further, not only can the just majority be trusted to "define the proper spheres of democratic authority," they *alone* may be trusted to do so. Any other arrangement would vest power and authority in a "will independent of the society."[32] Thus, the arrangement which Madison defended as avoiding both tyranny and anarchy, Judge Bork regards as courting tyranny whether by the majority or the minority. This is the context in which it is then alleged that evolved circumstances have produced a solution to the Madisonian problem—namely, the exclusive power of the judiciary to determine questions of rights and power in the United States. At bottom, therefore, the argument means that the original constitution failed, and the recourse to the Supreme Court has been a second line of defense, the very argument which Justice Thurgood Marshall offered in Hawaii in May of 1987:

The government they [the Framers] devised was defective from the start, requiring several amendments,

a civil war, and momentous social transformation to
attain the system of constitutional government . . . .

This essay does not maintain that Justice Marshall and Judge
Bork would entertain the same results as fulfilling their shared
vision of constitutional government. Further, Justice Marshall
has never uttered a word of the principle which Judge Bork went
on to affirm, that "any defensible theory of constitutional interpretation must demonstrate that it has the capacity to control
judges."[33] I do suggest, however, that the control Judge Bork
finally settled on is precisely no control at all. "The only way in
which the Constitution can constrain judges is if the judges
interpret the document's words according to the intentions of
those who drafted, proposed, and ratified its provisions and its
various amendments."[34] I submit that what this means is that
there is no constraint whatever, for the "only way" is a way which
leaves original intent jurisprudence no less open to the subjective
opinion of the judge than is the jurisprudence of evolutionary
utility. When Judge Bork goes on to describe the process by
which this constraint is to be accomplished, this conclusion
becomes still more manifest. He maintains that Dean Ely's
"discoverable premise" is the foundation. The jurist then adds a
minor premise designed to fit the original premise to contemporary circumstances, and *voila*, we proceed to a conclusion the
"framers could not foresee." Giving every due allowance to this
procedure and its announced intent to depart from the Constitution, it nevertheless remains true that the process of discover-
ing a premise is a step in ratiocination. It must accordingly follow
that this procedure aims to limit only the reason, not the power,
of the Court. Constitutional government, by contrast, must be
based on actual limitations on the power of the Court, for, among
other reasons, the fact that we all know only too well the
fallibilities of human reason.

Original intent spelled correctly would limit the power of the
Court, and that is the missing element in the contemporary

original intent debate. We grew up to believe that our judges, above all Supreme Court Justices, were clothed in the robes of the Constitution. Whether they wore anything beneath was of no importance. What counted was that they accept, as we believed, that our Constitution formed a government limited in *all* its branches and powers and that interpretation of that document would always start from the conceptions of its architects. When our judges cast off "a world that is dead and gone," in Justice Brennan's words, they cast off their constitutional robes and stand nakedly before us, asserting their own authority, independent of any limitations, to shape society as they will.

We have known for some time that *some* judges thought their power unlimited. Indeed Justice Powell made it explicit enough in a 1979 interview.[35] And Justice Marshall made the point clear in his 1976 Bakke opinion.[36] Nevertheless, Marshall was content to speak from the bench, and Powell's interview appeared only in an obscure college alumni bulletin, known generally only to a few scholars and lawyers. They did not enter the political thicket to make their nakedness a principle of right. What has been revealed, however, both gives pause and suggests a response. Discussing the earthshaking 1973 abortion decision[37] Powell declared, "There's nothing in the Constitution about privacy." Nevertheless, the Court invented a right of privacy to make their decision because, as Powell expressed it, "the liberty to make certain highly personal decisions [is] terribly important to people." Similarly, the Court says what the Constitution means, according to Powell, without relying on the intent of either Congress or the Founding Fathers. This they did, he held, when they invented the eighteen year old right to vote although "nothing in the Constitution . . . could have suggested that result." Simply put, "the Court decided that when young people were being drafted and asked to go to war . . . , the time had come to extend to them the right to participate as citizens in the decisions that affected them so seriously."[38] A review of how the

Twenty-sixth Amendment came to be passed would say far more than any commentary here could about the significance of this remark.

What this means is that our judges now stand in relation to the people of the United States where the judges of Abraham Lincoln's day stood in relation to the people of that era. When Lincoln challenged the people to consider whether they would accept a Supreme Court decision declaring slavery lawful throughout the United States, he meant for them to remember that that was their decision and not the decision of their judges. So, too, is today's American challenged by the tendency of contemporary Court opinions to make a decision how far they are willing to permit the Court to go. In the *Jaffree* decision on school prayer in Alabama,[39] the Court went so far as to mandate governmental neutrality between religion and irreligion. It is irrelevant whether it were *dicta* or law, in these premises, for in doing so they did more than merely to depart from the understanding of the Founding generation. They forced people to wonder, "What if they take the next step"; what if the Court insists that Americans cannot teach religion to their young, whether in public or in private because that has the effect of restricting what must be regarded as a highly personal decision which young people have a right to make for themselves? Would Americans abide a decision which would put their churches out of business and their faiths out of society?

Justice Brennan assumed just such a power in his speech of the fall of 1985.[40] That is at least a natural conclusion from his reason that there is no way for us to know what the Founders intended two hundred years ago. The more serious question, however, is what the American *citizens* of the Founding era intended, just as it is important to ask what Americans intend today. Brennan cited James Madison's changed opinion about the constitutionality of a national bank in order to persuade that the Constitution has no fixed meaning. Brennan erred in reading Madison.

Madison explained his changed opinion about the constitutionality of a national bank by pointing out that the decision to make such a bank was achieved by the very people who determined the Constitution itself. Therefore, their action constituted a legitimate interpretation of the *intention* of the founding in Madison's eyes. This pre-eminent Founder, in other words, considered the people far more the true founders than himself.

The Constitution does not need to change in order "to cope with current problems and needs."[41] As all the Founders so frequently said, the Constitution was intended as it stood to accommodate the needs of changing circumstances. By changing the Constitution we only make ourselves more vulnerable to changing circumstances. As drafted, the Constitution was intended to convey power sufficient to cope with transient problems without changing constitutional fundamentals. The theory was that in this way Americans would remain free; whereas in other states people change their constitutions as they change their garments. By Brennan's view, Americans should always regard the Constitution of the past generation as just so much dirty underwear.

Like Powell, Brennan defended the Court's decision to stand as a protector of the few against the many. In order to serve this role, the Court had to assume an independent power in the society, a position which Brennan conceded "requires a much modified view of the proper relationship of individual and state." In particular, the so-called "majoritarian process cannot be expected to rectify claims of minority rights that arise as a response to the outcomes of that very majoritarian process."[42] Brennan, like Judge Bork, believes that the Founders intended to create a simply majoritarian political order. Judging such an order unwise, he assumes the power and authority to change it.

It is characteristic in Brennan's argument that, when he makes his most radical claims, he reaches for the authority of the past to protect himself. Here again, he appealed to Madison. Here again, he abused Madison. Drawing from Madison's contribution to the debate on the Bill of Rights in 1789, he quoted that "the prescriptions in favor of liberty ought to be levelled against . . . the highest prerogative of power . . . the body of the people, operating by the majority against the minority."[43] Thus, Brennan used Madison to design a Constitution against the people.

The passage Brennan cited, however, follows a discussion in which Madison insisted that, in a government constructed such as ours, these declarations of rights (the Bill of Rights) do not "prevent the exercise of undue power" inasmuch as effective controls have been instituted in government itself. It is the community itself, not the "legislative body," which may profit from additional restraint, a restraint which derives from the "salutary tendency" of such declarations in regard to public opinion.[44] Thus, where Brennan found the idea of a Constitution against the people, we see in fact a description of those areas in which public opinion operates *outside* the so-called majoritarian processes. Madison remained consistent with what he had already said in defending the Constitution earlier, that "the rights of individuals, or of the minority, will be in little danger" from the government itself.

The beauty of this design was precisely that it made a government which did not have to create special categories of citizenship, dividing the society into legally created factions one against another, as our Court has done with whites and blacks, men and women, and other like divisions. The Founders *intended* a color-blind, class-blind Constitution. Our Court today intends the opposite. To restore the vision of the Founding, Americans would be forced to make the Court do again what Hamilton originally depended on it to do, "to declare all acts contrary to the *manifest* tenor of the Constitution void."[45] If the word "manifest" means anything at all, Hamilton must have understood that it is *not* the task of the Court to declare void legislation with which it merely happens to disagree.

Laying out the problem thus prepares us at last for the necessary conclusion. A knowledge of the Constitution sufficient to assure familiarity with its "manifest tenor" would exceed by far a literal rendering of its terms; it would reach to its principles as they were adopted and including the principles of the Declaration of Independence. Coupled with the demonstration that present-day jurists frequently miscomprehend the Constitution both in its terms and its principles, the likelihood emerges that the prospects for correctly spelled original intent depend on a complete renewal of the Court or something more still. This statement is not entertained lightly. We are tutored by present justices and judges themselves. Justice Brennan's abilities are clear in this regard. Similarly, Justice Marshall's disparagement of the Constitution bespeaks an unfriendliness to the understanding of republicanism articulated at the Founding. One might add that it also bespeaks an unfamiliarity with the Founding, for it is based on an erroneous reading of the attitudes toward slavery and blacks at the Founding. The general problem all of this raises is this: How far can we rely on the judgments of jurists who are neither well-affected toward nor particularly knowledgeable about the Constitution? If the principle constraint on the Court, subordination to the mechanisms and purposes of republicanism, is unknown to them, the justices cannot be expected to perform a function compatible with the political order. That is the real subject at the heart of the original intent debate.

It would be a mistake to rely on our Courts to fulfill the promise of original intent, since to do so would confirm in them a power far beyond anything originally intended. If such power in fact exists today, the American people would find themselves faced with no alternatives (to reclaim their due authority) but a constitutional limitation on the judiciary on the one hand, or, failing which, a revolution in their government. But it would be difficult indeed to imagine a constitutional limitation on the Courts, other than that in the original Constitution, that would be compatible with a government of laws. Could we recover a firm sense of the constitutional order, in which the separate authorities were regarded as properly independent where they were designed to be so, without having to appeal to a specific ruling of the Court for the purpose, that could perhaps restore the health of our polity? Fifty years of legislative complicity in judicial usurpation does not foster confidence in that possibility, however. Thus, for all practical purposes it would seem that an appropriate judicial deference on the one hand, or a righteous legislative and/or executive defiance of the Court on the other hand, are well beyond our reach.

What we can be most certain of is that this restoration cannot proceed from the Court itself. Justice Harlan's warning in *Oregon v. Mitchell* has gone all but unheeded not only by the Court but by the entire legal system:

> Judicial deference is based, not on relative fact-finding competence, but on due regard for the decision of the body constitutionally appointed to decide.[46]

Accordingly, Justice Frankfurter's insight, "There is not under our Constitution a judicial remedy for every [political mischief],"[47] counsels us to pursue other means. This consideration brings us nearer to the relevance of the idea of self-government in this discussion. Justice Brennan repeats no other phrase with such frequency as he repeats, without apparently understanding, "self-government." Since the original intent of the Constitution was to preserve self-government, however, it is most likely that the recovery of that heritage must involve the assertion of its claims over and against the institutions of the government, including the Court. That, in turn, would call upon a frankly political as opposed to a legal speech. This more than anything else could convey to us the impossible irony of seeking salvation in the Courts. For what would the judge be, who could speak with the accents the American people stand most in need of today?

Can we conceive some judge, attempting to refocus our constitutional deliberations, reminding the people that we don't need snivelling investigators and their pimps to tell us what our Constitution means? But such is the raw language of politics. He would continue: The people of this country are entirely capable themselves of insisting upon the due order of their Constitution. What we need are presidential candidates, for example, who can carry directly to the people the question of our Constitution—even to pose anew the question of their vote for the Constitution, whether the Constitution of Thurgood Marshall and Joe Biden or the Constitution of George Washington and James Madison. We need an executive who will not imagine that the way to defend the constitutional order is by cutting the budget of appropriately established governmental agencies and fighting over small bits of turf with an arrogant Congress. We need rather an executive who will lay down the general rule, that while Congress can carry out its appropriate authority to create policies, the president will carry out his authority to enforce its legislation—that the oversight responsibility of Congress is not only appropriate but encouraged, but that it does not consist in the right or authority of any congressman to sign checks. The executive himself will report to Congress, and Congress—individual congressmen and congressional staff—will not be afforded the opportunity to give immediate directions to the executive agencies of the government. We need an executive who will remind Congress that no individual congressman has a constitutional existence in this country—that congressmen come to light only as part of a constitutional majority, and that means a majority in the sense prescribed by the processes outlined in the Constitution. When they are deliberating and passing legislation, then they are invested with the full dignity of our republican system. As mere individuals expressing their likes and dislikes, they are just other Americans. It would take more than ordinary imagination to conceive of the Supreme Court opinion that would speak thus. Yet the restoration of the original intent hinges far more on such language than on the arcane disputes about the legislative records of the Founding era. Further, it is clear that the inadequacy of the Court is very closely connected with the malfunctioning of the entire federal government. What is genuinely cause for pessimism, however, is that it is almost as difficult to imagine such a political dialogue taking place off the Court as on it. In that event, Americans must face the cold reality that their options have been painfully narrowed to one only. Correctly spelled original intent may well demand original exertions.

## ENDNOTES

1. This essay was prepared at the request of The Federalist Society at Indiana University School of Law, Bloomington, and delivered before its "Symposium to Examine the Constitution at the Beginning of Its Third Century," entitled, "The Framer's Constitution: Dead Letter or Living Law?" The program was held on October 17th, 1987. A preliminary version of the lecture was delivered at Wabash College, October 16, 1987, in the Goodrich Lecture Series under the directorship of Professor Edward McLean.

Before I undertake the task of conducting a spelling bee on constitutional interpretation, I remind the reader of a familiar story which is inversely apposite to our present case. Geoffrey Chaucer's "Pardoners' Tale" relates the story of a small band of robbers who needed to cooperate among themselves in order to pursue their enterprise. They had to form a charter among themselves, agreeing that, though they would set forth on missions to stop wayfarers along the highway and rob them, they nevertheless would not rob one another. They would respect each the others' property rights once the booty had been distributed among them.

All who know the tale will recall that the robber band breaks up. It does so because, leagued as they are in the purpose to commit injustices, they had hearts which could not with respect to one another make the switch to acting justly. With poetic license, however, we may assume that the break-up did not come so quickly. Maybe it took six or eight generations before the fruits of injustice worked themselves out in their own souls.

Now we can witness an interesting problem: the problem of how to transmit the robbers' charter from one generation to the next. In the second generation, for example, one conceives that there would be in this robber band offspring of the first generation, carrying on their fathers' work, perhaps in much the same manner as their fathers had done. They would choose, as their fathers did, a boss to make decisions about targets of opportunity and lead them on successful forays. Of course, his henchmen would fall in line and carry out their part of the missions.

This would continue perhaps into the third generation, but eventually a creative boss would emerge. He might conceive that holding up travellers was a bit *declassé*. He would rather concentrate on bank robbing as more elegant, and perhaps even the profits would be more interesting. On his own authority he would decide that thenceforward they would only rob banks. There one has a community of sorts, and it has something of a constitution which designates someone to make decisions, to rule. He further decides what kind of activities they will participate in as a community. Bank robbing, however, is not so far removed from highway robbery.

The boss would perhaps manage without a challenge to his authority for making that decision. Time passes, however, and now, not in the time of the great-grandson but perhaps in that of the great-great-great-grandson, views might change still more. A boss might decide that robbing altogether is something of a bore and not very challenging. He might prefer to build the community inheritance by investing, managing portfolios, arbitraging.

At a remove of six or eight generations, a latter-day henchman might begin to ask questions. He might well say that his daddy was a robber, and his daddy's daddy in turn before him. He belongs to the community because he wishes to rob, not to invest. Hear him ask the boss, "Where do you get the right to tell me I'm going to invest?" The latter-day boss would probably respond by appealing to his authority (as well as general ideas about what's good for the latter-day henchman). He could say, "I inherited the right to decide from my daddy, who got it in turn from his daddy. The bosses have always decided, and what the boss decides the henchman must do."

Stretch this out in time and one sees a crisis emerging. It would be very unclear why anyone should listen to the boss, for the original intent of the robber band has become confused with the authority of the person making the decision. The original intent to rob has been lost sight of, as the boss appeals to his authority to decide (based on the needs of the day, to be sure) what it is that would be good for the community to pursue.

This story illustrates in the small the problem of constitutional interpretation. Reflection on how it is the robbers might come to understand or discuss authority, and how they might or might not settle this conflict, may well expand the scope of the discussion of original intent as it occurs among us today.

2. Benjamin Rush, "An Address to the People of the United States," *The American Museum* (1787).

3. Manuscript fragment, *Collector Magazine*, July 1892, p. 171.

4. Cf., Plato, *Crito*; Edward Samuel Corwin, *The "Higher Law" Background of American Constitutional Law* (Ithaca, N.Y.: Great Seal Books, 1955).

5. Raoul Berger, *Federalism: The Founder's Design* (Norman: University of Oklahoma Press, 1987).

6. Matthew Bacon, *A New Abridgement of the Laws of England*, Statute I (5) (3d ed., 1768), cited in Berger, p 16, n. 52.

7. Berger, p. 15-16, nn. 51-52

8. *Ibid.*

9. *Ibid.*, p. 194.

10. T. Cooley, *A Treatise on Constitutional Limitations*, 66-67 (2d ed. 1871), quoted in John H. Ely, *Democracy and Distrust: A Theory of Judicial Review* (Cambridge: Harvard University Press, 1980), pp. 18-19.

11. Berger, pp. 180-181.

12. Leonard Levy, *Judicial Review and the Supreme Court*, pp. 30-31 (1967), cited in Berger, *Id.* at 181.

13. Berger, *op. cit.*

14. *Garcia v. San Antonio Mass Transit Authority*, 469 U.S. 528 (1985).

15. 276 U.S. 394 (1928).

16. *Bowers v. Hardwick*, 106 S. Ct. 2841 (1986).

17. Reported in *Muskrat v. United States*, 219 U.S. 346; 31 S.Ct. 250; 55 L.Ed. 246 (1911).

18. *Marbury v. Madison*, 1 Cranch 137, 2 L. Ed. 60 (1803).

19. *Ibid.*

20. *Ibid.*

21. *Martin v. Hunter's Lessee* 1 Wheat. 304 (1816).

22. *San Antonio Ind. School Dist. v. Rodriguez*, 411 U.S. 193 (1973).

23. *Oregon v. Mitchell*, 400 U.S. 112 (1970).

24. *Ibid.*

25. Cf., Harry V. Jaffa, "What Were the 'Original Intentions' of the Framers of the Constitution of the United States?", 10,3 *University of Puget Sound Law Review*, 352-54 (1987).

26. *Saint Francis College v. Al-Khazraji*, 481 U.S. 604 (1987); rehearing denied 483 U.S. 1011 (1987) and *Shaare Tefila Congregation v. Cobb*, 481 U.S. 615 (1987).

27. 33 Daily Journal D. A. R. 1657 (1983).

28. 3 *Works*, 53-54, Letter to Henry St. George Tucker, December 23, 1817.

29. 3 *Works* 54-57, Letter to President Monroe, December 27, 1817.

30. "The Great Debate: Interpreting Our Written Constitution," speech reprinted by The Federalist Society, 1986, p. 44.

31. *Federalist* 51. in *The Federalist*, Jacob E. Cooke, ed. (Middletown, CT: Wesleyan University Press, 1961).

32. Cf., Allen, "Justice and the General Good: *Federalist* 51," in C. Kesler, *Saving the Revolution* (New York: The Free Press, 1987), 131-149.

33. Bork, *op. cit.*

34. *Ibid.*

35. With Professor Harry Clor, printed in the *Kenyon College Alumni Bulletin*, Summer, 1979, p. 14.

36. *Regents of the University of California v. Bakke*, 438 U.S. 265 (1978).

37. *Roe v. Wade*, 410 U.S. 113 (1973).

38. Clor, *op. cit.*

39. *Wallace v. Jaffree*, 472 U.S. 38 (1985).

40. "Address," to the Text and Teaching Symposium, Georgetown University, October 12, 1985.

41. Brennan, *ibid.*

42. *Ibid.*

43. *Ibid.*

44. *Annals of Congress*, v. 1, June 8, 1789; Reprinted in Helen Veit, Kenneth Bowling, and Charles Bickford, *Creating the Bill of Rights* (Baltimore: The Johns Hopkins University Press, 1991), especially pp. 80-82.

45. *Federalist* 78. In *The Federalist*, *op. cit.*, p. 524.

46. *Op. cit.*, at 207.

47. *Baker v. Carr*, 369 U.S. 186 (1962).

# Mother, God, and Federalism

RICHARD NEELY

The reason that I have entitled this paper "Mother, God, and Federalism" is that Federalism is one of those things—like Mother and God—that we are all *required* to love. Some of the most arcane but heated discussions at political science conferences concern the role of federalism in modern American government. Yet even those who, deep in their hearts, find federalism a bothersome anachronism will pay lip service to the principle. The legal literature is full of articles with titles like "The Death of Federalism," "The Second Death of Federalism," and "The Third Death of Federalism." I await next year's articles, "The Bride of Federalism" and "I Was a Teenage Federalism."

Whenever I become embroiled in academic discussions about federalism, it comforts me to remember a particularly elegant passage from Macaulay's *The History of England*:

> The science of politics bears in one respect a close analogy to the science of Mechanics. The mathematician can easily demonstrate that a certain power, applied by means of a certain lever or a certain system of pulleys, will suffice to raise a certain weight. But his demonstration proceeds on the supposition that the machinery is such as no load will bend or break. If the engineer, who has to lift a great mass of real granite by the instrumentality of real timber and real hemp, should absolutely rely on the propositions which he

finds in treatises on Dynamics, and should make no allowance for the imperfections of his materials, his whole apparatus of beams, wheels, and ropes would soon come down in ruin, and with all his skill, he would be found a far inferior builder to those painted barbarians who, though they never heard of the parallelogram of forces, managed to pile up Stonehenge. What the engineer is to the mathematician, the active statesman is to the contemplative statesman. It is indeed most important that legislators and administrators should be versed in the philosophy of government, as it is most important that the architect, who has to fix an obelisk on its pedestal, or to hang a tubular bridge over an estuary, should be versed in the philosophy of equilibrium and motion. But, as he who has actually to build must bear in mind many things never noticed by d'Alembert and Euler, so must he who has actually to govern be perpetually guided by considerations to which no allusion can be found in the writings of Adam Smith or Jeremy Bentham. The perfect lawgiver is a just temper between the mere man of theory, who can see nothing but general principles, and the mere man of business, who can see nothing but particular circumstances.

In my experience, arguments for federalism can be divided into three broad categories: (1) historical federalism, (2) result-oriented federalism, and (3) practical federalism. Of the three, the easiest to dispatch is historical federalism because it amounts to the type of pure theory that Macaulay so eloquently disparages. But there is little doubt that the men who drafted and ratified the Constitution of the United States did not envisage a strong, centralized, national government. The Constitution's framers and other professional politicians of the time might, indeed, have perceived the national government as potentially a stronger institution than the ordinary voter perceived it to be, but the need to amend the original document with a specific Bill of Rights to secure ratification shows how unenthusiastic the common people were about centralized power. All of that, however, was 200 years ago and historical federalism has been repealed by history. Much of that repeal occurred at the time of the Civil War when the Thirteenth and Fourteenth Amendments to the Constitution were passed, conferring broad new powers on the federal government. But the legal arguments based on minor changes in the constitutional document have less to do with historical federalism's repeal than a basic change in the way people perceive the federal government. Today public opinion polls show that the average voter thinks more highly of the honesty, capacity, and efficiency of the federal government than he does of either state or local government!

When today's political science professors point out that the federal government is a government of "delegated" powers, we all chuckle because by common consent state power has become more a matter of administrative convenience than an element of sovereignty. This has all happened painlessly since Franklin Roosevelt's first administration through the application of the "golden rule." Under the golden rule, whoever has the gold rules. And it is the federal government that can print money to finance any local activity from road building to school hot lunches. If the feds don't want us to drive faster than 55 mph in Wyoming or to drink below the age of 21 in New York, they need only tie the speed limit or drinking age to appropriations of federal highway funds and the states quickly pass accommodating statutes. The states are more interested in spending federal bucks than they are in preserving state sovereignty. To my knowledge no state (except, possibly, Arizona in one instance) has turned down federal money to stand on federalist principle! Therefore, if the states themselves aren't interested in principle, why should we be?

Furthermore, there is an understanding even among ordinary citizens of the problems inherent in fifty separate, sovereign, uncoordinated states. Thus, constituencies frequently repair to Congress to solve egregious problems that the states are incapable of solving. During the last two decades, as the divorce rate soared, both parental kidnapping and non-payment of support became serious interstate problems. The lack of coordination among state courts and the fact that state courts did not automatically accord full faith and credit to out-of-state custody decisions made it profitable for a parent to kidnap his child and flee to another state where, conceivably, that parent had good political connections. Similarly, in an economy where over 34 percent of all previously married, female heads of household are on welfare, collecting child support and alimony from defaulting husbands across state lines has become a major social problem. A deadbeat husband living in Massachusetts can cause California to spend $8,000 a year supporting his wife and children who may happen to live in California.

Less than half of the women entitled to child support or alimony get anything, and of those who receive something, less than 30 percent receive it all. Although the solutions that Congress has devised for these problems aren't very effective, Congress has taken action in both areas. The Parental Kidnapping Prevention Act sets forth specific standards to be applied by state courts in cases of interstate child snatching, and the Child Support Enforcement Act has tied tighter enforcement of child support to federal welfare appropriations.[1]

The history of the Child Support Enforcement Act is eloquent testimony to the fact that, notwithstanding whatever theory of decentralized government prompted the original constitutional vision, all of the practical conditions that underlay that vision have changed so dramatically that historical federalism no longer makes any sense. In this regard there will inevitably be the legitimate objection from formalists that the Constitution—our supreme law—must be literally enforced until properly amended. But honest lawyers have struggled with the problem of written laws that have not kept pace with changes in society since the dawn of legal science and, with perfect integrity, have developed principles for accommodating flexibility with the rule of written law. Perhaps the definitive statement on the subject may be found in Roman law in Book One of *The Digest of Justinian*, "De Legibus Senatusque Consultis Et Longa Constuetudine 32" where the following proposition is attributed to the praetor in the reign of Julian[2]:

> Age-encrusted custom is not undeservedly cherished as having almost statutory force, and this is the kind of law which is said to be established by use and wont. For given that statutes themselves are binding upon us for no other reason than that they have been accepted by the judgment of the populace, certainly it is fitting that what the populace has approved without any writing shall be binding upon everyone. What does it matter whether the people declares its will by voting or by the very substance of its actions? Accordingly, it is absolutely right to accept the point that statutes may be repealed not only by vote of the legislature but also by the silent agreement of everyone expressed through desuetude.

The second argument for federalism is what I call "result-oriented" federalism, which, notwithstanding its disingenuousness, generates the most die-hard political support. Result-oriented federalism is based on the simple phenomenon that, because the controlling constituencies at the state level are different from the controlling constituencies at the national level, state governments and the federal government give different political solutions to the same political problems. When I was young the most prominent incarnation of result-oriented federalism went under the sobriquet "states' rights." If a person was unenthusiastic about racial integration, the rallying point was simply that race relations were a matter best left to the states. And, obviously, the political structure of the southern states was such that little integration was likely to occur during lives in being plus twenty-one years. In the 1960s, of course, the liberal wings of both parties laughed states' rights to scorn, but those same folks would probably voice "federalism" objections today to a national law governing products liability simply because national law administered by life-tenured federal judges might be more favorable to business than current local law.

The idiocy of trying to make federalism into a useful concept in result-oriented debates can be seen from the vacillating positions that interest groups take on the subject simultaneously. For example, local governments lobby incessantly for more federal money for education. Yet local governments yell about a decisive blow to federalism when the Supreme Court rules that local governments must pay federal minimum wage to municipal transit company bus drivers. Similarly, the same plaintiffs' lawyers and criminal defense lawyers who have brought us racial integration, non-discrimination in employment, civil rights and civil liberties through federal court decisions using the Bill of Rights as the fulcrum scream like stuck pigs when it is suggested that federal courts might intrude into commercial matters under the Constitution's commerce or equal protection clauses. Result-oriented federalism, then, is simply a matter of political muscle combined with some quick conclusions about whose ox is going to be gored. Although result-oriented federalism is of enormous practical concern, it is unworthy of being taken seriously in terms of legal principles.

The third argument for a federalism, however—namely, practical federalism—is an argument worthy of the most serious and careful consideration. It is thought by many knowledgeable observers that much of America's efficiency, entrepreneurial dynamism, and upward mobility is directly related to the federal structure. Although it is impossible to summarize all the practical arguments for federalism here, the most important of them is that our federal structure inspires competition among *governments* in the same way that free enterprise inspires competition among private *businesses.*

Much recent economic literature points out that in every society political coalitions form for the purpose of affecting the distribution of wealth.[3] Mathematical models examining the logic of collective action demonstrate that distributional coalitions, such as labor unions, manufacturers' cartels, and populist political parties, are difficult to organize, but that once in place they are nearly impossible to dismantle. One (but only one) explanation for the remarkably unspectacular economic growth of Europe in general and England in particular in the last decade is that distributional coalitions have significantly impaired business incentives and distorted efficient resource allocation.

According to Professor Mancur Olson, who has written exhaustively in this area,[4] one reason why both Germany and Japan experienced extraordinarily high rates of economic growth in the 1960's (after post-war rebuilding was complete) was not that the war had destroyed their obsolete plants, but that the war had destroyed their distributional coalitions! Certainly history bears this out. The primary occupying power in both West Germany and Japan was the United States, and we imposed American ways of doing things on both countries during occupation. Among these American ways were broad-based industrial unions, discouragement of cartels, universal suffrage, labor mobility, civil rights, and unbridled free enterprise. After formal occupation, however, distributional coalitions again developed and began to exert political power, but they have taken different forms from what we currently see in England, France, and Sweden, where distributional coalitions have enjoyed long, uninterrupted historical evolutions.

This analysis becomes relevant to American federalism because much of the current geographical shift in the center of the American economy from North to South and East to West can be explained in terms of flights from distributional coalitions. At the simplest level there is a flight from traditionally unionized, high wage states like New York, Pennsylvania, and Michigan to traditionally low wage, non-unionized states like South Carolina, Florida, and Arizona. But the distributional coalitions that individuals can assemble for themselves, like labor unions, business cartels, and professional associations, pale in comparison to the distributional coalitions that can be established through government. Thus one strong argument for continuing a decentralized, federal structure is that when the federal government in the United States is a government of limited powers, it is state and local government that must be importuned to translate political power into all the various forms of wealth redistribution—ritualized job security, high wages unrelated to efficiency, social services, and social insurance.[5]

Part of our efficiency *vis a vis* England, France, and Sweden is that in America state governments must compete with one another exactly as businesses must compete. Studies of both state and national legislative elections disclose that there is a significant correlation between the level of employment and whether a political party will remain in power.[6] Furthermore, the ability of state and local government to reward their supporters with jobs and contracts, and to deliver on their promises about social services and public works is entirely dependent upon the tax base. Therefore, when both private job opportunities and the tax base are taken into consideration, distributional coalitions cannot extort the same concessions from the private sector in the United States that they can in European countries because here the extortee businesses will vote against the extorting locale with their feet. The point is perhaps proven by the fact that in France the socialist government of François Mitterand had to place

Draconian restrictions on capital flight (and even private travel) in 1982 to avoid an unfavorable foot ballot after the inauguration of traditional socialist programs!

A good example of the distributional coalition problem can be seen in the different rates of job creation in Western Europe and the United States. Under the guise of social justice, West European countries have created a two-tier economy that grants extensive protection to employed workers but makes it difficult for new workers to enter the labor market. A worker with a job in Western Europe enjoys great security and attractive wages, but there are few pressures to adjust wages and enhance job flexibility. In this regard, the British case is the paradigm. Despite an unemployment rate exceeding 12 percent, real per-capita earnings in Britain increased by roughly 3 percent between 1983 and 1985. In the first quarter of 1985, British labor costs jumped 6 percent!

During the 1970s, the anti-growth effect of distributional coalitions in Europe was obscured by unemployment rates that were lower than in the United States. But what was really happening was that total employment was declining because prime-age male participation rates were falling, the foreign labor force was being repatriated, and female participation rates were increasing only slowly. Thus, at the same time that America was creating millions of jobs—many for women and minorities—Western Europe had an absolute decline in employed workers.

Rigid dismissals legislation in European countries has transformed labor costs into fixed costs. When wage differentials were increasing between sectors of the economy in the United States and Japan from 1973 to 1982, they were narrowing in Western Europe, which meant that workers were not redirected from declining industries. Furthermore, in Europe there is more incentive than anywhere else in the world to substitute capital for labor. The distributional coalitions composed of *employed* workers who want high wages and strong security have created a rising relative cost of labor, and the rigid labor laws have discouraged the substitution of efficient workers for inefficient ones. At the same time, investment subsidies prompted by industry's political muscle have made investment in labor-saving equipment more attractive than investment in people.

But in the separate states of the United States the *threat* that segments of the job-creating, private sector will flee across state lines (or even abroad) has an incalculable tempering effect on both the militancy and effectiveness of distributional coalitions. And ironically, at least from the European point of view, one of the functions of the national government that has unconsciously evolved here in the United States is the evisceration by the national government of distributional coalitions at the state and local level. At the simplest level, this has meant the intrusion of the federal government into race relations in the South to avoid allocations of economic benefits on the basis of color. At a slightly more complicated level, federal control of bankruptcy establishes a perimeter around the perennial battles between debtors and creditors and creates a national, uniform system that is resistant to anti-creditor, populist urges.

Much of the theory of the current federal-state balance proceeds directly from the wisdom of *Federalist* Number Ten,[7] where it is pointed out that it is more unlikely that a faction (distributional coalition) will take control at the national level (where there are more balancing constituencies) than at the state level, where one narrow constituency (like farmers or industrial workers) can command a plurality. The genius of the federal structure, then, is that because most of the subjects that distributional coalitions wish to control (like job security) must be controlled at the state level, distributional coalitions are usually weak at the national level. But, exactly because the distributional coalitions are weak at the national level, it is often possible to use national law to weaken them even further when they attempt to dominate state and local government. This is the reverse of the classic vicious cycle; while the structural dynamics of centralized European countries tend to make distributional coalitions stronger and stronger, our dynamics tend to make them weaker and weaker. Thus, the dramatic decline in unionized workers as a percentage of the labor force in the last decade.

Fortunately, any theory of federalism—historical, result-oriented, or practical—has inherent limits that can logically be found in the structure of the Constitution of the United States itself. Although the Framers would not have expressed it this way, these limits proceed from the problem of "externalities." If either the benefits or the costs of a governmental action are experienced outside the jurisdiction where the action is taken, then it is logical to consign that issue to the national government. One instance of the problem of externalities specifically mentioned in the Constitution is defense. Were it not for the Constitution, Rhode Island could contribute nothing toward its own defense with impunity—just as Mexico contributes nothing to protect itself now—because states that choose not to pay their fair share for the defense of North America will still be protected to as great an extent as those that do by the states that choose to maintain military forces.

Modern life brings examples of externalities undreamt of by the Founders, such as factories in one state that pollute the air and cause acid rain to fall on the forests of other states, or a dam constructed in one state that causes rivers to dry up in another.[8] Even purist defenders of historical federalism concede that Congress can address the externalities problem.

There is one final rationale for practical federalism. This rationale is that small local government is more efficient than big national government. At the simplest level, getting a record from your local county courthouse is a surpassingly pleasant experience compared to getting a similar record from the social security administration, although like the county courthouse, social security has a local office nearly everywhere. Recently I have discovered that the federal government has two record process-ing centers—one a regional IRS office in Ohio and the other an INS visa processing center in Maine—that have *secret* telephone numbers. It is not just that the numbers are unlisted; it is apparently a high crime or misdemeanor for any government employee to disclose those numbers to anyone. Yet in state government you can get high ranking department heads on the telephone within a few days. In a state as small as West Virginia, any ordinary citizen can get an appointment to see the governor within two weeks. During my terms as West Virginia's chief justice, I talk *personally* to every person who calls my office! In the federal government you can't even get through to a G.S. 7 IRS or INS records clerk, much less a cabinet officer or commis-sioner.

In large countries with centralized, national governments the diseconomies of scale can be so acute as to be entirely laughable. In 1984 I spent a month teaching law at Fudan University in Shanghai where the students in my seminars discussed the then-current Chinese government structure. It turns out that one of the primary uses of the Chinese civil court system is to sort out contract problems between work units that are within the same ministry! The bureaucracy is so top-heavy that it is easier to settle a dispute between a bicycle manufacturer and a supplier of rubber tires about quantity, price, and delivery dates for tires in a court than it is to go up the chain of command to the person who is nominally the boss of both operations.

Unfortunately there are no firm conclusions that emerge from this brief horseback ride through a few of the high points of the federalism debate. But, perhaps, the very fact that there are no firm conclusions is itself a firm conclusion. It means, at least, that no rigid theory of federalism—particularly a historical one—is very useful for making the day-to-day decisions that end up dictating the contours of the federal-state system. Increasingly, the only practical way to answer any specific question concerning whether in a given case a national or local solution to a problem should be sought is simply to ask: "Is this a problem that is better solved nationally or locally?"

The universe of issues that are entirely "local" is shrinking every day. The example of how Massachusetts' unwillingness to enforce a child support award in favor of a California mother can cost California $8,000 a year is an illustration of growing "externalities" at the most basic level. But there are much more complicated and obscure examples of the externalities problem that theories such as historical federalism can't solve. For instance, in the typical products liability suit that proceeds in state courts the standard cast of characters include an in-state plaintiff, an in-state judge, an in-state jury, in-state witnesses, and a rich, out-of-state corporate defendant. In at least 22 states local trial court judges are directly elected in contested elections, which means that all the political muscle in the local court process (including appellate courts) is on the side of the in-state folks. It is hardly surprising, then, that the law of products liability becomes progressively more oriented towards simple wealth redistribution, and progressively less oriented towards a legitimate determination of such traditional issues as negligence, product misuse, or assumption of risk. For example, in one outstanding case, the operator of a tractor successfully sued the manufacturer for delivering a tractor without a roll bar in spite of the fact that the purchaser (the user's employer) ordered the roll bar removed before the tractor was delivered![9]

It quickly becomes apparent to anyone actively involved in products liability law that lack of coordination among America's fifty separate state court systems produces a "competitive race to the bottom" where each court system has but one option open to it—namely, to make sure that local residents get as much from out-of-state manufacturers as out-of-state residents get from in-state manufacturers. Yet this whole problem was entirely undreamt of by the Founders when they patched together a couple of million people living in 13 states where 80 percent of the population lived and worked on farms.

The problem for federalism is *not* that for rational reasons the federal government will progressively intrude itself into more and more areas of government. The real problem for federalism—particularly practical federalism—is that the national government will progressively intrude itself into more and more areas of government for *irrational* reasons. At the heart of the irrational intrusion problem is a complete revolution in political structures since 1913 when the Seventeenth Amendment to the Constitution was ratified allowing for the direct election of United States Senators. Before the Seventeenth Amendment, when senators were elected by the state legislators, the states *qua* states had a direct voice in the national government. Now United States Senators are largely elected through media blitzes funded by interest groups or wealthy individuals (such as Senator John D. Rockefeller, IV, himself) and neither senators nor congressmen need be much interested in how they represent their state governments as *governments.*

All of this is made worse by the decline of the local political machine in which local politicians from county commissioners through city mayors and state senators cooperated with U.S. Senators and Congressmen in a united party effort. Thirty years ago national politicians were directly dependent upon the good will of local officials for their own elections. Today that is not usually the case. Television, direct mail, and other technology allow direct interaction between national legislators and voters with the attendant result that national legislators find local officials more of a bother than an asset.

Given these dynamics it is surpassingly important that all our institutions of government—particularly the courts—remain vigilant in defense of the federal structure when it is being undermined for no good reason. If this paper stands for anything, then, it is simply that although both historical federalism and result-oriented federalism are red herrings, practical federalism is a vital, valuable, modern political concept. Practical federalism, then, is worth preserving. Preserving practical federalism, however, is more an exercise in pragmatic economic, sociological, political, and occasionally even scientific analysis on a case-by-case basis then it is an exercise in the application of some general theory that definitively solves every problem once and for all through a simple historical formula.

## ENDNOTES

1. In earlier periods such things as anti-trust, securities fraud, national unemployment insurance, and social security achieved high positions on the national legislative agenda.

2. It is worth remembering that Julian reigned in the late 4th century when the Empire was very old. After over 400 years of imperial history alone, Rome must have had an unbelievable body of obsolete law that had never been formally repealed but which was at odds with custom and usage in that age. For a good discussion of the general problem of obsolete statutes, *see* G. Calabresi, *A Common Law for the Age of Statutes*, Harvard University Press (Cambridge, 1982).

3. See, *e.g.*, M. Olson, *The Rise and Decline of Nations* (New Haven: Yale University Press, 1982).

4. *Ibid. See also* M. Olson, *The Logic of Collective Action* (Cambridge: Harvard University Press, 1971 ed.).

5. This is not to say, however, that all social programs designed to alleviate human suffering are necessarily foreclosed by the federal structure. Thus Title IX of the Social Security Act of 1935 (42 U.S.C. Section 1101) established a national system of employment security under which unemployed workers could receive state-administered unemployment compensation. The method used to achieve this desirable national goal was to impose a federal tax on employers (now levied under 26 U.S.C. Section 3301 *et. seq.*) unless a state levied its own employment security tax to establish a state unemployment compensation system. If the states failed to act, the federal tax was simply paid into the Treasury without earmark, but if the states established qualifying state employment security systems, 90 percent of the state tax was a credit against the federal tax. Mr. Justice Cardozo pointed out in *Steward Machine Co. v. Davis*, 301 U.S. 548 (1937) that the purpose of the federal tax was to avoid differences in manufacturing costs among the states so that states would *not* be discouraged from inaugurating employment security programs from fear that their industries would be placed at a competitive disadvantage.

6. For a quick summary, *see* R. Neely, *How Courts Govern America* (New Haven: Yale University Press, 1981) p.26, n. 2.

7. *Federalist* 10 was written by Madison.

8. The classic treatment of externalities may be found in R. H. Coase, "The Problem of Social Cost," 3 *J. Law & Econ.* 1 (1960).

9. *Hammond v. International Harvester Co.*, 691 F. 2d 646 (3rd Cir., 1982).

# The Life and Death of the Fourteenth Amendment and Its Federalism: Requiem for a Heavyweight

## WILLIAM F. HARVEY

Over seventeen years ago a law professor delivered a famous address in the Indiana University Law School at Bloomington. He commenced the address saying that constitutional law is persistently disturbing because of its lack of theory. This is manifest, he said, not only in the work of the courts but in "the public, professional, and even scholarly discussion of the topic." This means that courts are without effective criteria and that all of us expect that the nature of the Constitution will change as the personnel of the Supreme Court changes. This expectation is both inevitable and deplorable, we were told. In the rest of his address, in all of it, the remarks he made and the analyses he offered came in the hope that he might show that an absence of a principled constitutional analysis is both deeply disturbing as an intellectual quest, and that it has and might still inflict very great harm upon the democratic social order of the American Republic.

He said that his comments were not a general theory of constitutional law; rather, they "are more properly viewed as ranging shots, an attempt to establish the necessity for theory and to take the argument of how constitutional doctrine should be evolved by the courts a step or two farther."[1]

Seventeen years later his address became famous in the agony inflicted upon his life, in acts of savagery in the United States Senate. But the Senators would prove the central point: the

Constitution means almost nothing other than the personnel who sit upon the Supreme Court. As they change so does the Constitution: "You pays your money, and you takes your chances." One is put in mind of the comment made by Morris R. Cohen, the philosopher, who wrote to Professor Frankfurter: "The whole system is fundamentally dishonest in its pretensions (pretending to say what the Constitution lays down when they [the Justices] are in fact deciding what [they think] is good for the country)."[2]

The reply to Cohen, offered everywhere today, is that the Constitution created a Power Center, which in our tradition we still call the Supreme Court. The purpose of this Power Center is to choose values which are identified with the dominant group or groups and to superimpose them upon the American social order. The dominant group most certainly is not the same as a voting majority in a general election. It is very different. It stands in sharp contrast to Madison's majoritarianism. It is not a combination of shifting minority groups which, acting in momentary combinations, establish a legislative majority—this seems to be a favorite model in Departments of Political Science. The dominant group or groups are those to which the State has given enormous social and political power, and organizational and functional cash. With this they impose their Will.

Judge Robert H. Bork attempted to provide a principled alternative, even at the risk of being branded a "self-appointed scholastic mandarin" by Federal Judge J. Skelly Wright.[3] Judge Wright was attacking Professor Alexander M. Bickel, and all other members of the law school or general professoriate who might dare to suggest that the scholarly tradition permits criticism of the Supreme Court for its lack of principle.

The position I accept is that of the self-appointed scholastic mandarin. If this is in the tradition of Alex Bickel and Bob Bork, then I am very happy to share it.[4] In this, I come here to praise the Constitution, but not the Supreme Court; to remember what one part of the Constitution was, but is not today; to salute the genius of those men and women who understood and attempted to protect the elements of Liberty, in the Federalism of Section 1 of the Fourteenth Amendment.

When I think about our constitutional history, the thoughts are not those of today's Conservative or Liberal. The words "Historical Romantic" are appropriate. Here there is good company to share. Once we had a Constitution about which our sons and daughters could prophesy, and young men could dream dreams, and old men could see visions.

Professor William B. Allen's brilliant essay[5] instructs that Liberty rather than virtue was its organizing principle, because Liberty "called into being the idea of a state limited by the superior prerogatives of citizens."[6] Because of this the Constitution became "a genuine capstone of the American founding," and it fulfilled the promises of the Declaration of Independence. "[T]he Declaration's standard of equality and consent was preserved in the Constitution. To that end what was necessary was a Constitution truly reposing on the consent of the governed—one which recognized in the acknowledgment of equality that no human being had a title to rule over any other human being without his consent."[7]

These thoughts suggest an understanding about the achievement of 1868. It appears in the "Privileges and Immunities Clause" in Section 1 of the Fourteenth Amendment. If we are asked to identify the single most important clause in the Constitution of the United States, this is the clause, the place we look.

Liberty, and its elements, and Equality are derived from each person's inalienable right to consent. In 1789 this right established a Constitution and a limited federal government, but it was a Federalism in which power in the legislative function was almost unlimited.

Consistent with the structure of a limited government, a majority of representatives or judges could alter or remove elements of Liberty which the individual held. The majority might refuse to recognize the elements of Liberty except to the extent that they were protected, in Article IV's Privileges and Immunities Clause of 1789. This is a protection which extends to persons who are recognized as citizens. Citizens in that day did not mean all persons.

The adoption of the second Privileges and Immunities Clause in the Fourteenth Amendment made two great changes. First, it extended the elements of Liberty to all *persons*. The great research of Alexander M. Bickel, Charles Fairman, Raoul Berger, and many others shows part of the meaning of this Clause. It is that (1) there shall be no discrimination in civil rights or immunities, and (2) that every person of every race shall have the same right to make and enforce contracts, to sue and be parties and give evidence, to inherit, to purchase, lease, sell, hold, and convey real and personal property, and shall have (3) the right to enter a state, or to reside there, for the purposes of trade, agriculture, professional pursuits and (4) shall have claim to the writ of habeas corpus. Generally, these are the elements of Liberty.

Secondly, these elements of Liberty when placed in the Privileges and Immunities Clause of 1868 were made absolute. This understanding is central. When Professor Philip Kurland testified in the Bork hearings (which President Reagan called a "lynch mob"), he said that "no unencumbered right [is] in the Constitution, privacy or anything else." Kurland's testimony is a mistake of long-standing. These rights are absolute—they were placed beyond the power of the state, in any form, to affect or to invade. This is why the 1868 Amendment is great, and why it is unique. This is exactly what the authors of the Amendment intended; it is exactly what their words say. In this respect, the scholarship of Alexander M. Bickel, Charles Fairman, or Raoul Berger is deficient—it does not go far enough.[8] It was misled, and misdirected by the Supreme Court. So were we all.

This failure of understanding appears in every casebook on constitutional law used in American law schools. It dominates all discussion today. This terrible historical mistake assisted in denying Judge Bork a much-deserved seat on the Supreme Court. It denies all of us our Rights in Liberty which the Fourteenth Amendment was designed to protect. But it is much worse than this.

It is deadly serious, because the Court's error directly led to Jim Crowism and racial segregation for almost a century. This result came from the first great activist Court, the first non-originalist Court, the first statist Court, the first determinist Court, the Court which first disregarded the doctrine of original intent and became a Power Center. I suggest that we recognize the Judicial Mandarins for what they are, and to them give credit for what they have done.

If this is a "proclivity for extremism" which U. S. Senator Heflin found so troubling and threatening, then let us make the most of it.

We turn to things which are specific. Did the Privileges and Immunities Clause in the Fourteenth Amendment remove racial segregation from public schools, even though this existed in New York in the 1860s and in the District of Columbia? Of course it did. It made state-imposed racial discrimination impossible because the state could not adopt a statute or program which denied contractual alternatives to all persons. Racial segregation-discrimination is similar to slavery in one respect: it must have the power of the state in order to be established, and it must have control over persons who are imposed upon.

When persons exercise their absolute power of contract, and their right of mobility and residency, an effective, fully developed program or institution of racial segregation cannot occur. It is "not for nothing" that the first act of every Socialist regime since 1917, whether in Russia with Lenin or in Germany with Hitler, is the absolute destruction of the right to contract and the right to personal mobility. Their gulags would not exist if those rights, which do exist, were recognized.

Is there a right in a man and woman who have decided to engage in sexual intercourse to purchase an available contraceptive? In the Fourteenth Amendment there is. It is not found in some notion of a floating Right to Privacy. It is found in the Amendment's absolute Right to Contract. A state cannot adopt a statute which prohibits this contract, because it is beyond the power of the state. A state can adopt a statute that puts fetal killing beyond the competency of any person. This protects the Right to Contract in all persons, and it is permissible under the Fourteenth Amendment.

Those who wrote the Fourteenth Amendment, like Lincoln in their day, bet their all on those Rights. The institution of slavery, they knew, could not possibly survive the recognition of these Rights. Moreover, they also understood that no other system of restriction or restraint could arise because these Rights are absolute. Their work survived for five years: between 1868 and 1873.

In 1873 the first and probably the greatest non-originalist Court destroyed the Privileges and Immunities Clause in the Fourteenth Amendment. This occurred in the *Slaughter-House Cases*.[9] To this day it is the most significant decision since the Civil War. Its facts do not relate to racial discrimination. Its holding does. It removed the absolute right to contract: once removed or made subordinate to the power of the state, then all things became possible in the legislative halls. The first and lasting result was Jim Crowism and pervasive segregation in the United States. Each grew from the legislative power which was established in this decision in the Supreme Court. Neither is the product of the previous social crisis and condition known as ante–bellum slavery.

Two works of special note detail the rise and meaning of the *Slaughter-House Cases*. Dr. Lonn, in his work *Reconstruction in Louisiana*,[10] explains that a Bill finally passed the Louisiana Reconstruction Legislature, but over bitter opposition. It created a corporate monopoly over the slaughter of animals for human food in the City of New Orleans, and the parishes of Orleans, Jefferson, and St. Bernard, "after June 1, 1868." All other slaughter-houses were closed. This food production, consumed by perhaps 250 thousand persons, was a commerce of millions of dollars annually, in which men had worked for over a century. It was placed in the possession and control of one corporation and a few members in the Louisiana legislature who owned it.

Professor Charles Fairman gives a masterful presentation of the decision in the *Slaughter-House Cases*,[11] and it need not be repeated here. Justice Miller for the 5-4 majority held that the rights found in the Privileges and Immunities Clause came from the State (either a state government or the federal government). Moreover, only national citizenship received recognition from the Privileges and Immunities Clause, and national citizenship did not comprehend any of the fundamental rights of the individual or the person referred to in the Amendment.

The great Rights which were absolutely protected in the Privileges and Immunities Clause in 1868 had become unknown to the Court in 1873, and very soon in the legislative halls in the nation. They were replaced by Power. The Federalism placed in the Fourteenth Amendment disappeared. Now a mere majority at any time might disregard rights entirely, and for all time.

Justice Miller and his majority thought in terms of Power. They refused to understand that the principal purpose in the Fourteenth Amendment was to deny power over fundamental rights to the State, whether a Legislature or a Court, or whether in the Congress or the Supreme Court. The duty of the State is to protect those Rights. This much power it has and no more.

Justice Miller and the Court did not comprehend the essence of the Declaration of Independence or the Constitution itself: the Rights of Liberty do not derive from and are not allocated among state power centers. Their creation is not in state power, whether legislative or judicial.

The dissents in *Slaughter-House* were correct. In part they said that if the right to choose in the context of one's freedom of contract were placed into a state-created caste, then "hereditary" factors would determine if a trade or a profession would be closed unless pursued by one's father.

And so it was. In 1890 five conventions were held to attempt to determine what might be done. These conventions were attended by blacks who were observing the walls of governmental discrimination being built. They were built on the denial and the destruction of their rights to contract and to mobility and residence which occurred in the *Slaughter-House Cases*.

This decision of 1873 commenced the doctrinal approval of governmentally-imposed racial discrimination. It took only 25 years for Jim Crowism to reach full bloom. The Court's decision in *Plessy v. Ferguson*,[12] also from the State of Louisiana in 1896, was inevitable.

Today there is truth in Professor Cohen's charge: the Supreme Court's law depends on the personnel on the Court. But the Constitution does not. It is not that the Fourteenth Amendment, with its magnificent Privileges and Immunities Clause, based initially on the Civil Rights Act of 1866 and mainly on the Declaration of Independence, has been tried and found wanting. It is that it has not been tried at all.

The first Republican president said, "Ours is a nation dedicated to a proposition . . .," but Lincoln's principles and their central liberating theory were removed from the 1868 Constitution by the Supreme Court. The Court destroyed the central meaning and purpose of the 14th Amendment and replaced them with Power—its Power.

Judge Bork was correct when he spoke as a professor in 1971. He was correct when he testified as a judge in 1987. His intellectual integrity meant that he would become a victim in the "biggest power game in town." And so he was. Homer Adolph Plessy, an earlier victim of Power, would understand.

## ENDNOTES

1. Bork, "Neutral Principles and Some First Amendment Problems," 47 *Indiana Law Journal* 1 (1971).

2. Quoted in Berger, *Government by Judiciary*, (Cambridge, MA: Harvard University Press 1977), p. 416, fn. 31. In 1967, A.A. Berle published a short work called *The Three Faces of Power* (New York: Harcourt, Brace & World). His thesis is that the Supreme Court of the United States is a revolutionary committee: "This second phase was the really revolutionary development—and, incidentally, set up the Supreme Court as a revolutionary committee." *Ibid.*, at 10. Berle did not object that the Court functions in this way. He said that it was not avoidable, and that it pleased him.

3. Wright, "Professor Bickel, The Scholarly Tradition, and the Supreme Court," 84 *Harvard Law Review* 769 (1971).

4. Mandarins indeed! It would be difficult to find two law professors more openly involved in the issues of our time than Alexander M. Bickel and Robert H. Bork. It is not possible, I suggest, to find two law professors who have contributed more to our understanding of these issues. At the time of his death Alex Bickel was a personal friend, and we were working on two briefs together, one in the Supreme Court and one in the U.S. Court of Appeals for the Seventh Circuit. They were filed and bear my name. I shall always be proud of his contribution to them, and of his warm and private praise for them.

5. Allen, "Liberty's Hour: The Constitution in the Revolution," 7. *Lincoln Review* 11 (Spring 1987).

6. *Ibid.*, at 14.

7. *Ibid.*, at 15.

8. This mild criticism of these very great scholars is offered with profound respect for them and their work. This element, that these Rights are absolute and beyond the power of the State to affect, is very clearly the expressed intention of Congressman John A. Bingham, who is credited as the author of Section 1 of the XIVth Amendment. It is shown in his discussions of Section 1 of the XIVth Amendment; Section 1 of the Civil Rights Act of 1866, Ch. 21, 14 Stat. 27 (1866); ;and Section 7 of the Freedman's Bureau Bill, cited in McPherson, *Political History of the United States* (New York: Philip Solomons, 1871), pp. 73-74. The discussions may be found in part of the *Congressional Globe*, 39th Cong., 1st Session, House, p. 2542. Other leading scholars, such as James, Collins, Gressman, Flack, Kurland, Graham, Corwin, Tenbroek, and Cooly, have missed the central purpose in Section 1 of the Amendment. All of the reasons for this are beyond the scope of these "ranging shots." One clear reason, however, is the Supreme Court's insistence that the meaning of the Privileges and Immunities Clauses where they appear in the Constitution is unclear. This is little more than a Power-serving myth, but it is insisted upon as in *Baldwin v. Montana Fish and Game Comm'n*, 436 U.S. 371, 380 (1978).

9. 83 U.S. (16 Wall.) 36 (1873). Compare *Butcher's Union Co., v Crescent City Co.*, 111

U.S. 746 (1884).

10. Lonn, *Reconstruction in Louisiana after 1868*, (New York: G. P. Putnam's & Son, 1918).

11. Charles Fairman, "Reconstruction and Reunion 1864-1888," *History of the Supreme Court of the United States, VI*, (New York: Macmillan Co., 1971). The serious student of this subject is invited to read Fairman's superb judicial biography of Justice Miller in *Mr. Justice Miller and the Supreme Court, 1862-1890* (Cambridge, MA: Harvard University Press, 1939).

12. 163 U.S. 537 (1896). Again a recommendation: the careful student should pursue the brief for Homer Adolph Plessy, whose attorneys understood the Fourteenth Amendment, as did Justice Harlan in his dissent. In part the brief said:

> We insist that the State has no right to compel us to ride in a car 'set apart' for a particular race, whether it is good as another or not. . . .
>
> The question is not as to the *equality* of the privileges enjoyed, but *the right of the State to label one citizen as white another as colored in the common enjoyment* of a public highway as this court has often decided a railway to be.
>
> Neither is it a question as to the right of the common-carrier to distinguish his patrons into first, second and third classes, according to the accommodation paid for. This statute [the Jim Crow Act from the Louisiana Legislature] is really a restriction of that right, since the carrier is thereby compelled to provide two cars for each class . . . . In fact, its plain purpose and effect is to provide the white passenger with an exclusive first class coach *without requiring him to pay an extra fare for it.*

(All emphases in the original brief.)

There is remarkable historical irony and tragedy here. Mr. Plessy's attorneys made this argument thirty years after the Civil Rights Act of 1866. The argument is almost exactly the same as the explanation of the Act, and later, Section 1 of the XIVth Amendment. Professor C. Vann Woodward explains that in the 1880s racial discrimination was often erratic and inconsistent. In the old seaboard states of the South such as Virginia, he tells us, Negroes were free to ride first class as whites. The age of Jim Crow was yet to come, and it arrived with a legislative vengeance in the 1890s. Garraty, *Quarrels That Have Shaped the Constitution*, Chapter X by C. Vann Woodward, on "The Case of the Louisiana Traveler," p. 146 (New York: Torchbook, Harper & Row, 1964). In those conditions, Mr. Plessy's plea for principle and for a principled interpretation of the Constitution was as unavailing as it is today.

# The Separation of Powers: Myth or Reality?

PASCO BOWMAN

The purpose of these remarks is to examine the functional significance of the separation of powers doctrine in our constitutional plan of government. I also wish to consider the treatment the doctrine has received from the Supreme Court and other institutions of government, and to inquire into the current status of the separation of powers. Is the doctrine alive and well, functioning pretty much as the Framers intended it should, or is it essentially moribund? Is the separation of powers myth, or reality? In this brief paper I will not provide anything like a truly definitive or comprehensive view of the doctrine, but I will give you my impressions and my present views.

As a starting point, we need to look at the framework of the Constitution, and consider the place of the separation of powers in the constitutional scheme of things. The Framers had as their general goal the creation of a national government with meaningful power. Their view, shared by many of their contemporaries, was that the central authority established under the Articles of Confederation was inadequate to safeguard the interests of the new nation, and that a stronger central government was needed. At the same time, having only recently overthrown the oppressive British rule, they were very much aware of the dangers of unlimited governmental power, and also of the potential for abuse when too much of *whatever* power the government has is concentrated in the same hands. They did not want a government strong enough to destroy freedom and independence, nor did they want another George III. Their task, then, was a tricky one: To create a government with real power, but not too much, and with that power spread around rather than concentrated in one place. Checks and balances, an idea derived from Britain's mixed form of government, was well known to the Framers. So was the doctrine of the separation of powers, as developed by Montesquieu in his classic work, *The Spirit of the Laws*. He defined political liberty as "a tranquillity of mind, arising from the opinion each person has of his safety." How to achieve political liberty? Montesquieu's answer is that political power must be divided. "When the legislative and executive powers are united in the same person," he says, "or in the same body of magistracy, there can be then no liberty." "Again," he continues, "there is no liberty, if the power of judging be not separated from the legislative and executive powers." He prescribes that the legislative power itself should be divided between a lower house representing the common people and an upper house represent-ing, in Montesquieu's words, "persons distinguished by their birth, riches, or honors." The executive must have the veto power, and may propose legislation, but otherwise must have no part in the making of laws. The legislature must have no share of the executive power, but although the legislature, said Montesquieu, "has no right to stay the executive, it has a right and ought to have the means of examining in what manner its laws have been executed." Of the three powers, he says, "the judiciary is in some measure next to nothing," for the judges should be no more than "the mouth that pronounces the words of the law." But he also says, "Miserable indeed would be the case, were the same man, or the same body whether of the nobles or of the people, to exercise [the] three powers, that of enacting laws, that of executing the public resolutions, and that of judging the crimes or differences of individuals."[1]

Americans of the Revolutionary era tended to embrace

Montesquieu's ideas. Indeed, the separation of powers doctrine was reflected in all the state constitutions of that time, finding its most forceful expression in Part the First, Article XXX of the Massachusetts Constitution of 1780, which states:

> In the government of this commonwealth, the legislative department shall *never* exercise the executive and judicial powers, or either of them; the executive shall *never* exercise the legislative and judicial powers, or either or them; the judicial shall *never* exercise the legislative and executive powers, or either of them; to the end that it may be a government of laws, and not of men. (emphasis added)[2]

This is the apparent origin of our proud boast that ours is "a government of laws and not of men"; significantly, this language is appended to an explicit separation-of-powers provision.

There can be little doubt that the Framers of the Federal Constitution, like those of the Massachusetts Constitution of 1780, viewed the principle of separation of powers as indispensable to political liberty. In Number 47 of *The Federalist*, Madison wrote that "[n]o political truth is certainly of greater intrinsic value, or is stamped with the authority of more enlightened patrons of liberty."[3] And of course, the separation of power principle did find its way into the Constitution, even though it is not mentioned there by name.

Though not explicitly recognized, the doctrine of separation of powers is expressed in the Constitution in the first section of each of the first three articles. Article I, Section 1 provides that "*[a]ll legislative Powers* herein granted shall be vested in a Congress of the United States, which shall consist of a Senate and House of Representatives." Article II, S 1 provides that "*[t]he executive Powers* shall be vested in a President of the United States of America." Article III, S 1 provides that "*[t]he judicial Power* of the United States, shall be vested in one Supreme

Court, and in such inferior Courts as the Congress may from time to time ordain and establish." (emphasis added)[4]

While focusing on the separation of powers, I pause to note some of the other ways in which the Framers sought to protect political liberty. Although all legislative power is assigned to Congress, Congress is divided into two houses. (Indeed, this is a further separation of power within the legislative branch.) Congress's powers are enumerated, *i.e.*, the permissible subjects upon which it may legislate are defined.[5] Moreover, certain subjects are put off limits, *i.e.*, the Constitution specifies certain things Congress may not do, *e.g.*, no bills of attainder or ex post facto laws shall be passed, no money shall be drawn from the Treasury but pursuant to appropriations made by law, no title of nobility shall be granted by the United States, etc.[6] Limits also are placed on the power of the states, *e.g.*, no state shall enter into any treaty, or grant any title of nobility, pass any law impairing the obligation of contracts, coin money, etc.[7] Implicitly, all other matters, except for those powers explicitly conferred upon the national government, are reserved to the states—a point later made explicit by the Tenth Amendment, adopted as part of the Bill of Rights in 1791. The Bill of Rights, of course, places further substantive limitations, indeed very important ones, upon the powers of the federal government.

The overarching plan is clear: a national government of limited powers, with those powers divided among the three branches, each with a different function and different personnel, and all of this in the context of a federal system in which a large amount of the totality of all governmental power would be reserved to the states. Through this limitation and dispersal of power, the Framers hoped that liberty could be secured, that our country would have in fact a government of laws and not of men.

Montesquieu, writing in the eighteenth century, observed that "[m]ost kingdoms of Europe enjoy a moderate government," because to at least some degree their governments reflect a separation of powers. "In Turkey," he adds, "where [the] three powers are united in the Sultan's person, the subjects groan under the weight of tyranny and oppression."[8] We can make, validly, the same observation about the world of the twentieth century. It may be said with little fear of contradiction that wherever the separation of powers principle is practiced it promotes limited government, political liberty, and respect for human rights, and that where the separation of powers does not exist, where all power is held either by law or in fact by one monolithic organ of state, the subjects groan, just as in Montesquieu's day, under the weight of tyranny and oppression. As recently pointed out by Justice Scalia, dissenting in *Morrison v. Olson*, the independent counsel case, which I will come back to later, "[w]ithout a secure structure of separated powers, our Bill of Rights would be worthless, as are the bills of rights of many nations of the world that have adopted, or even improved upon, the mere words of ours."[9]

Mere words, even those of a Constitution, are not self-executing, whether what is at stake are the freedoms protected by a Bill of Rights or the dispersal of power sought by the separation of powers principle. The Framers recognized "[t]he insufficiency of a mere parchment delineation of the boundaries" to accomplish a true separation of powers.[10] "The great security," said Madison, "against a gradual concentration of the several powers in the same department consists in giving those who administer each department the necessary constitutional means and personal motives to resist encroachments of the others. The provision for defense must in this, as in all other cases, be made commensurate to the danger of attack."[11]

Madison reasoned further that, in republican government, the legislature is necessarily the predominant branch. Thus, it must be divided into two branches, with, as he puts it, "different modes of election and different principles of action, as little connected with each other as the nature of their common functions and their common dependence on the society will admit."[12] On the other hand, the executive branch, because of its relative weakness—it can only enforce laws, not make them, and it does not have the power to tax—must be fortified. Therefore, the veto power, and the Framers' rejection of proposals to divide executive power by having multiple executives, or by having a council of advisors with separate authority. Therefore, the conferral upon the president of the power to appoint, with the advice and consent of the Senate, ambassadors, judges of the Supreme Court, and all other officers of the United States whose appointments are not otherwise provided for in the Constitution.

This, in a nutshell, is the constitutional allocation of power given to us by the Framers: Separation of powers among the three branches, with a few checks and balances to prevent any branch from abusing or exceeding its power with impunity. Each branch was to have its own powers, and was not to encroach on the powers of the other branches. As we already have seen, the Framers were cognizant of the danger of such encroachment. They could only hope that the ensuing years and our unfolding history would see maintained the allocation of power among Congress, the President, and the courts in such a way as to preserve the equilibrium the Constitution sought to establish, so that, in Madison's words, "a gradual concentration of the several powers in the same department" can be avoided.[13]

How has it turned out, this grand experiment? Have we remained faithful to the original vision? The answer, I believe, is a qualified yes. In the actual workings of our government, and in our Constitutional jurisprudence, the separation of powers is more than myth. It is real; it is built into our Constitutional structure; it is a force to be reckoned with. Still, there are some troubling signs, developments that are, I believe, cause for concern. I will come to those momentarily.

First, I would observe that I believe the Framers would be very surprised—and taken aback—by the expansive view that has been taken of the enumerated powers in Article I. Separation of powers issues aside, the federal government is far larger, more complex, more powerful, more expensive, doing more things, and more intrusive into the affairs of the states and the lives of the people than anything the Framers could have envisioned or that they gave any hint of having intended. Similarly, I have a feeling they would be quite surprised—and taken aback—by the powers exercised by the judiciary, which the Framers, along with Montesquieu, regarded as the weakest and least dangerous of the three branches. It now is in some ways the dominant branch, exercising a sweepingly broad jurisdiction primarily as the result of the Supreme Court's expansive reading of certain portions of the bill of rights and of the post-Civil War amendments, and also as a result of the broad scope the Court has given to the "case or controversy" requirement of Article III. An argument certainly can be made that the Supreme Court's self-generated expansion of its power to decide cases, together with its expansive reading of the Constitution, has encroached not only on the Executive and Legislative branches, but also upon the powers of the states, thereby helping to throw the federal system out of balance by effectively shifting power from the states to the national government in a way none of the Framers could have foreseen. All of these things, and more, I believe, would startle the Framers and would prompt them to ask us some searching questions. *E.g.*, they might ask, "Have you made a conscious decision to establish this enormous, interventionist, intrusive national government, or did it just happen while no one was looking?" Or, "How do you propose to keep this gargantuan state under control? How can you be sure it will remain (if it is) your servant and not your master? How can something this large, complex, and pervasive truly be a government of laws and not of men?" Or, "Is your government attempting to do so many things for so many people that it can no longer give proper attention to the essential functions of a national government?" All these questions, and others, doubtless would occur to the Framers.

Returning to our theme, how is the separation of powers doctrine faring these days? I have said that it remains far more than myth, but that some troubling developments have occurred. I now turn to these.

First, we cannot fail to note the growth of the independent administrative agencies—agencies created by law that are outside of the President's direct control. (*E.g.*, FTC, FCC, SEC, etc.) Such agencies wield great power, operate under broad legislative authority, and tend to pursue their own agendas, without a great deal of effective review by any of the three established branches. They are not provided for in the Constitution, but have been justified by constitutional theories that it would unduly prolong this paper to discuss. These agencies typically not only make rules and enforce them, but also decide their own cases. Thus legislative, executive, and judicial powers are combined in the same agency, which necessarily takes on the attributes of a government within a government. The cases adjudicated by these agencies are subject to review in the federal courts, but the scope of review is narrow, with great deference given to the agency's fact-finding and also to its interpretation of doubtful points of law arising out of the statute or statutes that the agency administers. The availability of judicial review may be enough to keep the agencies honest and faithful to the task Congress has set for them, but their internal structures and combination of powers, together with their effective removal of executive power from the President, are very much at odds with the principle of separation of powers.

As a second area of concern, I would suggest that our recent history has seen an expansion of congressional power and a concomitant loss of presidential power. Examples from three areas of conflict between Congress and the President will illustrate the point.

First, foreign affairs. Article I, Section 8 grants Congress the power to regulate commerce with foreign nations, to define and punish offenses against the Law of Nations, and to declare war. In all other respects, the Constitution leaves to the President the authority to conduct the foreign affairs of the United States. In part, the Constitution does this expressly. Article II, Section 2 empowers the President to make treaties, with the advice and consent of the Senate, and he is charged with the duty of receiving ambassadors and other public ministers. The rest is by necessary implication. The conduct of foreign affairs was well-recognized as necessarily a part—a supremely important part—of the executive function, and the Constitution does not indicate in any way that the Framers had the unlikely intention to assign this responsibility to either of the other branches. Congress, however, when dissatisfied with the policies of the President in foreign relations, has displayed an increasing propensity to get into the foreign affairs game and to attempt to micromanage foreign policy. While I do not denigrate Congress' motives, the result of this propensity, it seems to me, is a lack of coherent policy in foreign affairs (since we speak with too many voices), a sense of unease among our allies (are we reliable? can we be depended upon to follow through on commitments and to finish what we start?), and a diminishment of the President's legitimate authority to safeguard American interests in a volatile, rapidly changing, and sometimes hostile world.

Judicial appointments are a second area of conflict between Congress and the President. An intense fight was waged over the nomination of Justice Rehnquist to the office of Chief Justice. In 1987, when the President nominated Judge Robert Bork to fill the vacancy created by the retirement of Justice Lewis Powell, the battle reached a fever pitch, and the President lost. This of course was not the first time that the Senate has voted down a nomination to the Supreme Court. President George Washington saw one of his nominees, John Rutledge, rejected for political reasons by the Senate, with votes against the nomination being cast by several senators who had been delegates to the Constitutional Convention, as had Rutledge himself. What was exceptional and disturbing about the defeat of Judge Bork was not the fact that the Senate ultimately rejected the nomination, but that the struggle took on so many of the characteristics of an election campaign. TV commercials, newspaper ads, direct mail, massive expenditure of funds—all these means and more were employed to discredit the nominee in the eyes of the public and to put political pressure on Senators who were otherwise inclined to confirm the President's nomination. As is well known, much of this was orchestrated by members of the opposition party in the Senate. The effect was not only to degrade the entire process, but to alter radically the traditional balance of power struck by Article II, Section 2 of the Constitution between the President and the Senate in the appointment of Article III judges.

A third area of recent conflict between Congress and the President with separation-of-powers implications centers on the laws passed by Congress during the post-Watergate era for the appointment of independent counsels to investigate and prosecute misconduct within the executive branch. Under the Constitution, enforcement of the laws is a function of the executive branch. Neither Congress nor the Courts have any authority in this respect. However, may Congress require the executive to appoint an independent counsel to look into alleged wrongdoing within the executive branch and, if wrongdoing is found, to prosecute the wrongdoers, with the independent counsel acting in all of this outside the operational control of the President? This question came to a head in *Morrison v. Olson*, decided by the Supreme Court in June 1988. The answer of the Court was yes, such a law is constitutional. The Court specifically held that the act in question (the Ethics in Government Act of 1978) does not violate the principle of separation of powers by unduly interfering with the executive branch's role, even though the Court conceded that the functions performed by the independent counsel are executive functions, and even though the President's only real control over the independent counsel is, through the Attorney General, to remove the counsel for "good cause." In dissent, Justice Scalia characterized this minimal control as a "shackles" on the President rather than "an effective means of locomotion." The majority, however, viewed this as an effective control and was willing to validate the Act, concluding that the Act gave the executive branch enough "control over the independent counsel to ensure that the President is able to perform his constitutionally assigned duties."[14] This appears to be a way of saying that the Constitution permits Congress to chip away at the executive power so long as the President, in the opinion of the Court, retains enough power to do his job. The majority thus took a highly pragmatic and flexible view of the separation of powers, as opposed to the strict view advanced by Justice Scalia. Whichever side is correct, chalk up another win for Congress, another loss for the President.

This, of course, is not the first time a President has lost a constitutional struggle involving the separation of powers doctrine. President Truman lost the case involving his seizure of the steel mills during the undeclared war in Korea, and President Nixon lost both of his cases involving control over his presidential papers. Nor is this the first time the Court has taken a pragmatic, flexible approach to a separation of powers question. Indeed, that was the approach adopted by the Court in *Nixon v. Administrator of General Services*,[15] upholding an act of Congress (signed by President Ford) directing the Administrator of GSA to take custody of President Nixon's presidential papers and have them screened by government archivists.

In looking back over the Supreme Court's decisions on separation of powers issues, one does not find a high level of consistency. While at times it has taken a flexible approach, at other times it has taken a strict view of the separation of powers. Examples of the strict approach include *Chada v. INS*[16] (striking down the legislative veto of executive branch action), *Northern Pipeline*[17] (holding that the judicial power of the United States may be exercised only by Article III judges; hence statute authorizing bankruptcy judges created under Article I to exercise the powers of Article III judges in bankruptcy matters must fall—legislative judges cannot substitute for judges with full attributes of Article III); and *Buckley v. Valleo*[18] (separation of powers doctrine prohibits Federal Election commission with members appointed by Congress from discharging executive functions, which can be performed only by "Officers of the United States" appointed as provided in the Constitution). Similarly, in *Bowsher v. Synar*,[19] the Court held that the powers vested under the Gramm-Rudman-Hollings Budget Control Act in the Comptroller General, who may be removed only at the initiative of Congress, violated the constitutional separation of powers principle that Congress play no direct role in the execution of the laws.

That the Court has been inconsistent in applying the separation of powers principle to the cases that come before it is hardly surprising, for neither were the Framers of one mind or one voice on the question of strict versus flexible separation of powers. To the extent that the Constitution mixes powers and creates shared powers, it does so in the interest of creating effective checks and balances and thereby preventing the abuse of power. Indeed, Professor Forrest McDonald, in his magisterial work *Novus Ordo Seclorum*, flatly concludes that the doctrine of a rigid separation of powers had clearly been abandoned in the framing of the Constitution.[20] The text of the Constitution—*e.g.*, the President's veto power, the shared appointments power—demonstrates the correctness of that conclusion. Such a conclusion in no way suggests a clear answer to any or all of the difficult and diverse separation of powers cases that flow into the courts and that must be adjudicated by them, but at least it counsels moderation and a balanced perspective. I can think of no better way to close this paper than with a quote from Professor McDonald:

> [I]n an ultimate sense the Constitution did reflect a Montesquieuan principle, perhaps the most fundamental of them all: it provided for a government that would itself be governed by laws, and by laws that conformed to the genius and circumstances of the people.[21]

The essential task, then, for us, the living, the inheritors of the legacy bequeathed by the Framers, is to remain true in this fundamental sense to the original intent, so that power remains divided, liberty is preserved, and we can continue to boast with justifiable pride that ours is, not merely in words but in fact, a government of laws, and not of men.

## ENDNOTES

1. Charles de Secondat, Baron de Montesquieu, *The Spirit of the Laws*, Book XI, Chapter 6, par.6.

2. Constitution, State of Massachusetts, (1780).

3. Madison, Federalist No. 47, in *The Federalist*, John C. Hamilton, ed. (Philadelphia: J.B. Lippincott & Co., 1873).

4. Constitution of the United States of America. In my text, I have underscored "all legislative Powers," "the executive Power," and "the judicial Power" in order to emphasize the *exclusiveness* of these grants of power. The Constitution could not be clearer that each of the three branches is granted *all* of the power of the federal government in that branch's respective field, subject only to such sharing or mixing of powers as is specified in the Constitution itself.

5. Article I, Section 8.

6. Article I, Section 9.

7. Article I, Section 10.

8. Montesquieu, Book XI, Chapter 6, par. 6.

9. *Morrison v. Olson*, 487 U.S. 654, 697 (1988) (Scalia, J. dissenting).

10. Federalist No. 73, Hamilton.

11. Federalist No. 51, Madison.

12. *Ibid.*

13. *Ibid.*

14. *Morrison v. Olson*, 487 U.S. 654, 696 (1988) (majority opinion).

15. 433 U.S. 425 (1977).

16. 462 U.S. 919 (1983).

17. 458 U.S. 50 (1982).

18. 424 U.S. 1 (1976).

19. 478 U.S. 714 (1986).

20. Forrest McDonald, *Novus Ordo Seculorum: The Intellectual Origins of the Constitution*. (Lawrence: University Press of Kansas, 1985). p. 258.

21. *Ibid.*, p. 260.

# The Family and the Constitution

## ALLAN CARLSON

Our federal constitution departs from a pattern found among other written constitutions in the Western world: it gives no attention to the institutions of marriage and family. The Constitution of the Fifth French Republic, for example, makes lofty promises about defending the interests of the family, as does the Basic Law of the Federal Republic of Germany, as did the Constitution of the Weimar Republic before it.

But marriage and family are not mentioned in our Constitution. Indeed, the original document is even fairly clean of gender-identified language; at times, it reads as though it were edited by the staff at *Ms.* magazine. That awkward word, "person," is used whenever the generic word "man" would have sufficed, and the Founders dutifully avoided any family-oriented language, such as "head of household," to define those holding the franchise. Rather, such decisions were left to the states.

In part, family issues are avoided in the U.S. Constitution because they were irrelevant: the document is a compact between thirteen sovereign states, designed to solve a given set of political and economic problems that had surfaced under the Articles of Confederation; the status of the family was not among them.

More broadly, though, the family was deeply embodied in the unwritten constitution of the new United States, in the social views that the Founders held. Indeed, I would argue that their work *rested* on assumptions about the social order that need underlie a free republic, assumptions about the sort of people they were dealing with, and about the way that we citizens would live. In all the celebrating that marked the bicentennial to the U.S. Constitution, recognition of this "unwritten constitution" was largely absent.

It is desirable to describe the social order—the family system—that the founders assumed would exist as the foundation of their enterprise. I will give particular emphasis to the importance of the family economy, or the home economy, if you will. My attention will then turn to the process though which we have dismantled large shares of this family economy: in the nineteenth century, through the growing influence of an alien, statist ideology; and in the twentieth century, through the regular surrender of the Tenth Amendment to the waxing power of the Fourteenth Amendment.

The social history of the constitutional period has been dominated by the Whiggish, or liberal, interpretation, which gives emphasis to American exceptionalism, the American difference. In his 1960 book *Education in the Forming of American Society*, Bernard Bailyn offered the classic argument, saying that the New World environment, alive with prospects of abundance and expansion, promoted the rise of a unique individualism. From the earliest settlements, "the ancient structure of family life," shaped by strong networks of kin and community, eroded in America, and the family retreated towards its marital core of man and woman. Meanwhile, the instability of the frontier situation promoted frequent migration. Out of this, concludes Bailyn, the modern American emerged, marked by a "sense of separateness" and a heightened individuality, that stood in sharp contrast to the kin-oriented peoples of old Europe.[1]

Variations on this argument also appear. In his detailed 1960 study of the frontier town of Kent, Connecticut, historian Charles Grant found a colonial population of proto-entrepreneurs, with little sense of community or family loyalty. This was "a population raised on an economic tradition of land speculation and individualistic venturing," he reports, and they refused to make sacrifices for any cause other than themselves. As Grant puts it, "One sees in certain of the Kent settlers not so much the contented yeoman,...but perhaps the embryo John D. Rockefeller."[2] More recently, Jay Fliegelmann's *Prodigals and Pilgrims* uses literary sources to document what he calls "the American revolution against patriarchal authority," arguing that our Founders translated their rebellion against Parent Country and Patriarchal King over to their private lives, and so crafted a social revolution against the bonds of the traditional family.[3]

The central problem with this interpretation, though, is its teleological thrust: the suggestion that American history has been a process of goal-directed evolution, toward individualistic liberalism—as the engine of history ground along, all else fell aside.

But a new kind of social history has emerged over the last twenty-five years, challenging this view of the Revolutionary and Constitutional periods, and giving a very different understanding of the place of the family in this critical phase of nation's past. Borrowing research questions and techniques from the French *Annales* school of historiography, these historians have offered a much richer, and decidedly different, portrait of America in the 1770s and 1780s. Rather than a nation of individualistic entrepreneurs and speculators, they see a land characterized by age-stratification and patriarchal power, by strong kin connections and ethnic and religious communities, and by a household mode of production bonded to subsistence agriculture: in short, an America much closer to the hierarchical family systems of Europe than previously supposed.

This social system dominant in the late 18th century could be defined by five qualities:

(1) *First, the primacy of the Family Economy.* A few joint stock

companies aside, most Americans in the late eighteenth century organized their economic lives around the family in the home. They arranged their labor along family lines, rather than through a wage system. Most productive activities—from furniture construction and candlemaking through the raising and preparation of food—were family based. As the family gave symbolic and emotional meaning to subsistence activities, its own essence was shaped by the home-based character of production. Indeed, "family" and "economy" formed a rough unity in this time, and family relations were conditioned by economic questions of property and labor. This family economy involved a complex web of obligations: parents enjoyed legal possession of property—as freeholders, tenants, or sharecroppers—and counted their own children as both dependents and workers through the culturally set age of majority. In turn, these adults were dependent on their children for economic support in old age, and focused great attention on the terms and timing of the transfer of economic resources to the succeeding generation.[4]

In this home-centered economy, men and women held quite different, although complementary, tasks, all necessary for the survival of the family unit. Largely self-sufficient households, drawing supplemental help from a local exchange network of neighbors and kin, remained the focus of the lives of the vast majority of Americans well into the nineteenth century.[5]

(2) *The second dominant quality of late colonial social life was the continued power of kinship and ethno-religious communities.* New studies focused on towns and counties show the influence of local ethnic groups and religious bonds over many aspects of daily life. One paper studying York County, Pennsylvania, for example, reveals the varying life patterns of Ulster Presbyterians, German Lutherans, and English Quakers within the same small region. Differences in economic and inheritance patterns between the communities are contrasted with the persistence of those pat-

terns over many generations.[6] Ethnic groups also formed closed economic communities: every name in the 1775 account book of shoemaker-butcher Henry King of Second River, New Jersey, was of Dutch origin; similarly, the main business connections of the Jewish, Quaker, and German merchants in Lancaster, Pennsylvania, were, without exception, with their respective coreligionists in Philadelphia.[7]

(3) *The third quality of American life was the central focus on land.* The founding generation shared one overriding concern: land, particularly the preservation of the family landhold into the future. In his study of Quaker farmers in the Delaware Valley, Barry Levy found a population committed to the creation of families and the rearing of children, as "tender plants growing in the Truth." Land was their central focus: not as a speculative venture, but as the necessary foundation for a godly home. As these families acquired larger estates, the motivation was a "child-centered use of land." Indeed, the family served as a kind of revolving fund, shifting land resources between generations over the life cycle.[8]

Looking at Andover, Massachusetts, Philip Greven, Jr., describes "the consuming concern" of fathers to see that their sons were settled upon the land, for land possession represented their core value. Daniel Snydacker describes farms and families in late-colonial America as "two halves of a corporate whole."[9] James Henretta emphasizes the central goal of the American population as the preservation of an agricultural society of yeoman, free-holding families. Such farms, moreover, were not capitalist enterprises, but were devoted rather to subsistence agriculture. In the 1790s, regional studies have shown, only 15 to 25 percent of farms produced enough surplus to engage in market transactions. Due to lack of markets and transportation networks, as well as to cultural preferences, the large majority of farms produced enough to feed the resident family, and a little for barter with neighbors and kin, in a non-cash system of local exchange based on crude "just price" theories. In the Middle and North colonies, hired farm labor was rare: the account books of these families indicate that they invariably chose the security of diversified production, rather than carrying the risks of hiring non-farm labor and producing for sale.

Economic gain, while important to Americans, was not the overriding concern: it was subordinate to the long-run security, in land, of the family unit. Toward this end, the central goal of fathers was to craft farms for their children that were viable economic units. Even widow's rights—notably the customary "widow's third"—were made subordinate to the protection of the estate. Property, in effect, was "communal" within the family, aiming at preservation of the land for posterity.[10]

(4) *The fourth social quality of late colonial American was the abundance of children.* In its reproductive patterns, the new United States was the equivalent of a modern Third World country: a demographic hot house, swarming with children. In 1790, one half of the whole population was age 15 or younger, a phenomenon seen today only in places such as Kenya. One reliable estimate has a U.S. Total Fertility Rate in 1800 of 7.0, meaning that the average woman of that generation bore seven children (by way of comparison, the current TFR is 1.85). Recent studies suggest that fertility had fallen in the North American colonies between 1700 and 1725, partly in response to wars in Europe, and partly due to constraints on new settlement. Yet between 1725 and 1800, fertility climbed again to historic high levels. A new fertility decline, while evident in some scattered groups shortly after 1775, did not occur on a widespread basis until well into the nineteenth century.[11]

Children in America, though, were more than the accidental product of the sexual act, or precious bundles to care and nurture. They were also economic assets to their parents and extended

134 DERAILING THE CONSTITUTION

families, new laborers for the family enterprise and sources of security for the care of the old. No less an observer than Adam Smith, in his *Wealth of Nations,* published in 1776, remarked that the rapid economic growth in England's American colonies both reflected and rested on the abundance of children: "Labour [in North America] is...so well rewarded that a numerous family of children, instead of being a burden is a source of opulence and prosperity to the parents. The labor of each child, before it can leave the house, is computed to be worth a hundred pounds clear gain to them....The value of children is the greatest of all encouragements to marriage. We cannot, therefore, wonder that the people in North America should generally marry very young."[12]

These perceptions, moreover, were no illusions. Recent studies of both colonial Deerfield, Massachusetts, and contemporary Egypt confirm the point: in agriculture societies without the apparatus of a welfare state, children deliver tangible economic assets over the parents' life cycle, both in terms of wealth accumulation and security in old age.[13]

(5) *The fifth quality of the colonial social order was the power of inter-generational bonds.* Late eighteenth-century America was age-stratified, with older men using their control of financial resources—above all, land—to secure and maintain status and power. Age, not class, appears to have been the principle agent of social control. The young men were relatively powerless; the old used elaborate methods of gifts and bequests to bind their children to them. Widows usually remained dependent on their children, through a complex mix of inheritance and customary services in kind. As one social commentator has put it, parents raised children to "succeed them," not merely to "succeed." Through this orientation, the agricultural family remained a lineal one. While each generation lived in separate households, the nature of production and methods of inheritance bound these nuclear units through many ties. Duties and rights criss-

crossed the generations. As one historian has put it, "the line was more important than the individual; the patrimony was to be conserved for lineal reasons."[14]

These five qualities—the primacy of the family economy, the continued power of kinship and community, the central focus on land, the abundance of children, and the power of inter-generational bonds—defined the social order of America in the years before, during, and immediately after the Revolution and the drafting of the Constitution. With particular strength in the agrarian societies of the North and upland South, the lineal family stood at the center of American economic and social existence. Judging from the evidence of diaries, letters, and wills, it is clear that most men, women, and children viewed their world through this prism of family values, and the same evidence suggests that it shaped the assumptions through which the Constitution writers worked. They understood the family unit as setting the constraints on the individual; as forcing a balance between the person's quest for power and goods and the needs of the community and posterity. This family-centered world put limits around private ambition, the entrepreneurial spirit, and even religious membership. The Founders assumed that most American eyes would be turned toward home, which would deliver ordered society within a regime of liberty. And they also assumed that the home must have an economic base to it: that it could not survive as the center of moral power if it was stripped of its economic significance.[15]

Defense of this social order, this society of households, lay with the states, and the people. The federal Constitution presumed a nation of families, and ultimately relied on the Bill of Rights, specifically the Ninth and Tenth Amendments reserving the rights of the people and the power of the states, as the primary bulwarks against social experimentation. Unfortunately, they did not prove to be enough.

The American family system faced new challenges in the early

19th century, particularly in New England. The expansion of markets and early industry made the payment of wages more common, leaving sons less dependent on fathers, fathers less dependent on sons, and families less reliant on home production. The growing influence of land speculators, bankers, and mortgage companies also disturbed assumptions about land and family that had bound together the social order.[16]

The factory system posed the greatest challenge to the family system. For two generations, though, technological factors in league with cultural pressures kept industry within the home. Through the 1830s, the family factory—involving production for market sale and the application of the division of labor— remained dominant. This system of home work, or household manufacture, drew female labor into the market economy without dislocating the family as the center of economic life. This, in turn, preserved the reciprocal economic bonds between parents and children.[17]

However, in the South, the family system of the United States remained strong, with no sign of significant challenge through the whole period up to the Civil War. In this region, the family served as the main source of personal security, advancement, and assistance. Definitions of selfhood sprang from one's family ties; personal ambition and glory rested on survival of the family name and patrimony, and their promise and heritage for the unborn. The individual sought immortality through blood ties, not through the accumulation of goods or power. As John C. Calhoun explained, "The Southern States are an aggregate of communities, not of individuals." The family, with the father and husband at its head, was the agency for setting daily routine, defining social conventions and deviance, and setting the lines of social order. Believing that power belonged in the home, Southerners battled the encroachments of other institutions—government bureaucracies, common schools, and even national church bodies—that threatened family order. By 1860, for example, the average child in the mid-Atlantic states spent 157 days in school; in the South, only 80 days, a fact reflecting the common view that the family, not the school, should be the bearer of ideals to the young, particularly through oral tradition and example. Even the peculiar Southern custom of marriage between cousins was driven by the desire to preserve and, if possible, extend the family patrimony and to ensure personal security. This family system was also pro-natalist, or pro-birth, by social convention, and honor adhered to having a family with numerous children. At the same time, the great fear haunting antebellum Southerners was the danger of becoming a ward of the state. In short, as historian Bertram Wyatt-Brown has concluded: "What nineteenth-century whites [in the South] claimed to be, they actually were—a people devoted on the whole to founding families, sometimes creating princely lines by their standards, and preserving elemental distinctions of blood . . . and gender."[18]

Since the 1840s, though, American social history could be written as the deliberate dismantling of the home-centered economy, and the consequent decay of the foundations of our liberty. Except on the margins, this turn against the home was not a natural consequence of industrialization or the emergence of a modern economy. Rather, the change derived from the application of statist ideology and consciously-made political and legal choices.

The first direct assault on family autonomy grew out of the reform school movement during the 1830s. These institutions, centered in the early years in New York and Pennsylvania, took poor and so-called "neglected" or "delinquent" children from parents, and placed them in institutions, to—it was said— "prevent" them from entering a life of crime. In 1839, the Pennsylvania Supreme Court declared such actions constitutional. Twisting an ancient concept of English chancery law designed to protect the estates of orphaned minors, the court established a new doctrine in American law: *parens patriae*, literally, "the parenthood of the state." Justifying the termination of parental rights, the justices stated: "May not the natural parents, when unequal to the task of eduction or unworthy of it, be supplanted by the *parens patriae*, or common guardianship of the community?"[19] This elevation of the state over the family rapidly expanded into one of the greatest usurpations of American liberties yet devised by the Courts. As the Illinois Supreme Court ruled in 1882:

> It is the unquestioned right and imperative duty of every enlightened government, in its character of *parens patriae*, to protect and provide for the comfort and well-being of such of its citizens as, by reason of infancy, defective understanding, or other misfortune or infirmity, are unable to take care of themselves. The performance of this duty is justly regarded as one of the most important of governmental functions, and *all constitutional limitations* must be so understood and construed so as not to interfere with its proper and legitimate exercise.[20]

Through legal logic of this sort, the family was stripped of elemental legal protection.

The same spirit animated the public school movement, and the compulsory education laws that gave it power. Horace Mann and his fellow common school enthusiasts sought to use state education to "socialize" the new immigrants in Massachusetts into a special mix of religious Unitarianism and political liberalism. At a deeper level, the school reforms cut into the fabric of the family economy, stripping children of a large share of their economic value and removing parents from control of their offsprings' uprearing.[21]

The proponents of state schooling were rarely shy about their motives. As one South Carolina school inspector, in arguing for a compulsory attendance law, explained: "The schools exist primarily for the benefit of the State rather than for the benefit of the individual. The State seeks to make every citizen intelligent and serviceable." He mocked concern about "the sacred rights and personal privileges" of parents who kept their children at home: "The State has the right to carry the lawbreaking child to the reformatory or to jail to protect society. Has not the State as much right to carry the child to the school . . . to train him to benefit society? Those who deny the right of the State to compel the parent to send his child to school are too frequently the offending parents themselves, sentimental theorists or vacillating politicians."[22]

Court decisions on the constitutionality of compulsory attendance laws placed parental rights as secondary to both the "welfare of the minor" and the interests of the state. According to the Indiana Supreme Court in a 1901 decision, the natural rights of a parent to the custody and control of his infant child were subordinate to the power of the state. In this vein, the school attendance law was not only constitutional, but "necessary" to the very purposes of the Constitution itself.[23] A related decision in Pennsylvania argued that the public had "a paramount interest" in the virtue and knowledge of its members, and "of strict right" the business of education belonged to the state. Accordingly, the educational function of the family not only could be, but *should be* stripped away. Significantly, the Pennsylvania justices referred with admiration to recent U.S. Supreme Court interpretations of the Fourteenth Amendment, particularly the new view of law as "a progressive science," which must always alter a settled principle with an expansive interpretation that would meet "advancing and changing conditions."[24]

Indeed, the twentieth century bore witness to the progressive sacrifice of the U.S. Constitution's Tenth Amendment, granting reserve powers to the States, to both the growing sweep of the Fourteenth Amendment, and to the burgeoning welfare state. The press for a federal child labor law, for example, rested again on the conscious repudiation of states rights, "parental rights," and the "family economy." Parents' control over the training and future of their children, advocates said, must be subordinated to the higher interests and higher wisdom of the central state. Individual states allowing parents flexibility, particularly offenders in the South, would have to be brought into line.[25]

The crafting of the old-age benefits portion of the Social Security system also aimed at dismantling another aspect of the home economy: inter-generational security. In its 1935 report to the President, the Committee on Economic Security noted that "children, friends, and relatives have borne and still carry the major costs of supporting the aged." But the committee used the circumstances of "the present depression" to push for a state system that would, over time, replace family insurance with social insurance.[26]

Legal challenges to the Social Security system focused on the Tenth Amendment, and the charge that the new laws violated rights reserved to the states. The U.S. Supreme Court, though, rejected the argument, using the economic crisis to sweep aside the states' rights complaint. More importantly, the Court also referred to that bastard legal concept, the parenthood of the state, as justification for the new welfare mentality: "The *parens patriae* has many reasons—fiscal and economic as well as social and moral—for planning to mitigate disasters that bring these burdens in their train."[27]

Federal family welfare laws have also subverted the economic integrity of the family. While the spirit had been growing for decades, Herbert Hoover's 1930 White House Conference on Child Health and Protection marked the triumph of a new conception of the State's child. The 1909 White House conference, enthusiasts noted, had mainly aimed at deinstitutionalizing orphans and delinquent children; and the 1919 conference had focused on child labor. But with the 1930 assembly, they noted cheerily, "the [state's] emphasis swung very definitely from dependent and handicapped children . . . to all children, of *the whole family of the nation,* wherever they lived and whatever their situation." Indeed, one semi-official product of the conference described a new entity: "Uncle Sam's Child," a product "who belongs to the community almost as much as to the family," a "new racial experiment," and a citizen of "a world predestinedly moving toward unity." The same volume attacked the rural home and the rural family—legacies of the old vision—as psychologically inadequate, while praising public schools as "a community power with more potential influence for orienting the child to his environment than any other."[28]

This new spirit further undermined the economic foundations of family life. At first, federal welfare programs seemed traditionalist in intent. Indeed, the 1935 report of Roosevelt's Committee on Economic Security defended the proposed Aid to Dependent Children program as an affirmation of stay-at-home motherhood: "[These measures] are designed to release from the wage-earning role the person whose natural function is to give her children the physical and affectionate guardianship necessary not alone to keep them from falling into social misfortune, but more affirmatively to rear them into citizens capable of contributing to society."[29] But, in fact, this new measure merely represented another step in dissolving the natural family economy, by separating women from the need for a bond to men when raising children. Indeed, by the latter 1970s, the system was fully skewed toward support of the modern mother-state-child family, to the exclusion of fathers. The state had become the breadwinner. Economists Lowell Gallaway and Richard Vedder found that until a child reached age 12, welfare benefits actually exceeded the cost of raising a child; by the time the child reached age 17, benefits exceeded costs by $3,000.[30] At the same time, the U.S. Supreme Court struck down attempts to condition public assistance on "marriage" or "family" status, arguing that the denial of benefits to persons in new or novel lifestyles violated the "equal protection" standards of the Fourteenth Amendment.[31]

The U.S. Supreme Court's recent rulings on the meaning of marriage have followed a similar course, undermining the family economy. In 1888, the Court described marriage as "something more than a mere contract . . . . It is an institution, in the maintenance of which in its purity the public is deeply interested, for it is the foundation of the family and of society."[32] As late as 1965, the Court recognized in *Griswold v. Connecticut* that "marriage is a coming together for better or worse, hopefully enduring, and intimate to the degree of being sacred."[33] But in 1972, a mere seven years later, the Court used the logic of the Fourteenth Amendment to strip marriage of any meaning, arguing that "the marital couple is not an independent entity with a heart and mind of its own, but an association of two individuals each with a separate intellectual and emotional make up." Accordingly, marriage could no longer have a preferred status.[34]

The federal income tax has also been altered in recent decades in an effort to tax residual home production. The 1972 expansion of the income tax deduction granted to parents using day care, the substitution in 1976 of the Child Care Tax Credit, and the special tax credit given to two-income married couples in 1981 were all designed—at the expert level—as a way of indirectly taxing the services of the mother-at-home: her labor in areas such as child care and food preparation. For the first time, the Internal Revenue Service successfully invaded hearth and home and imposed an indirect tax on the intimate exchanges within the private family economy.[35]

If the Founders of this nation were correct, if the unwritten constitution was important to the definition and preservation of a free Republic, then we are in deep trouble. Assumptions about the family basis of social order and economic exchange have been subverted by a statist ideology that has elevated the State above the family, and by the prevailing interpretation of the Fourteenth Amendment, which has undermined the ability of the Tenth

Amendment to defend states and their inhabitants against intrusions by the national government.

Again, if the Founders were right, recent changes in law should have contributed to rising measures of social disarray, and this is what we see. The number of annual divorces in the U.S. tripled between 1960 and 1981, rising to 1,213,000. The number of children annually affected by divorce more than doubled. With the economic logic of marriage under siege, the rate of first marriage declined by 30 percent; among women ages 20-24, the fall was an astonishing 60 percent. With children stripped of any economic value, the birth rate tumbled in half, from 118 (births per 1000 women, ages 15-44) in 1960 to only 65 in 1978. Meanwhile, as illegitimate births drew extensive state subsidy, their number more than tripled, from 224,000 in 1960 to 715,000 in 1982.

Moreover, there is compelling evidence that these dramatic changes in American social life are linked, in turn, to a rise in juvenile crime, a sharp increase in the incidence of drug abuse, the decay in the educational performance of youth, a sharp rise in youth suicide, and (in part) soaring levels of health care costs.[36]

So what should be done? In order to preserve the bases of liberty, our current need is to rebuild the natural family economy, as best we can. We can act on the assumption that the current situation was not inevitable, nor the result of some immutable law of capitalism or of history, as Karl Marx would have it. Rather, our modern social crisis derives in large part from conscious political interventions, made in the past, that can now be altered.

A practical agenda designed to recover the home economy as the foundation of our Constitutional order would include:

(1) *Tax reform that ends the taxation of home production, while affirming marriage and children.* That would mean eliminating the existing Child Care Tax Credit, or universalizing it,

by granting a fixed tax credit to all parents with pre-school children. It would also involve a sharp increase in the dependents deduction for children (from the current $2,000 to, say, $4,000), and creation of a new Dependent Child Credit, keyed to family size, that would, in effect, rebate a large portion of the payroll tax paid by parents with children.

(2) *Second, housing policy that restores the linkage of family to the land.* In the seventeenth century, Quaker immigrants left England and settled in rural Pennsylvania, hoping that "it might be a good place to train up children amongst sober people and to prevent the corruption of them here by the loose behavior of youths and the bad example of too many of riper years."[37] In the twentieth century, Americans have migrated again, from the cities to the suburbs, the latter an Anglo-American invention designed to reconcile rural life with the modern order and specifically designed to shelter and protect children.[38] While a nation of yeoman farmers is no longer practical, a nation of families on independent homesteads is, and one of the few instances of successful social policy found in our past are the housing programs of the federal government that operated in the 1940s and 1950s. Housing policy should again aim at opening opportunities for home ownership among young couples, including special, low-interest mortgages and the creation of IRA-like housing accounts.

(3) *And third, measures that return economic activities to the home.* This strategy would include changes in school laws, giving more protection from interference to that rapidly growing group of Americans: home schoolers. Over one million American children are now taught at home, by parents laboring to restore a primal aspect of the family

economy.

This strategy would also involve continued efforts to eliminate federal, state, and local regulations that limit the kind of labor that can be done at home. The Reagan administration began the process, by loosening regulations on some forms of handwork. Much more needs to be done, as we find ways for both women and men to make a living within the family domicile. Recent innovations in computer technology, along with renewed interest in handwork and crafts, make the family economy possible again, for those who choose to live by its rules.

In sum, the survival of our liberties and of our constitutional order may depend on our ability to turn back a century of statist corruptions and to rebuild at least certain aspects of a home-centered economy. The Founders understood the family to be the social unit that reconciled liberty with order, that kept the individual's interests in balance with the interests of community and posterity. We have already paid a huge price for forgetting that lesson, a price that ranges from high levels of crime to environmental degradation. The proper response, at both the policy and personal levels, is *a turn toward home.*

## ENDNOTES

1. Bernard Bailyn, *Education in the Forming of American Society: Needs and Opportunities for Study* (Chapel Hill: University of North Carolina Press, 1960), pp. 15-36.

2. Charles S. Grant, *Democracy in the Connecticut Frontier Town of Kent* (New York: Norton, 1961), pp. 53-54, 170-71.

3. Jay Fliegelman, *Prodigals and Pilgrims: The American Revolution Against Patriarchal Authority*, (Cambridge: Cambridge University Press, 1982), pp. 5-6, 263-67.

4. James A. Henretta, "Families and Farms: *Mentalite* in Pre-Industrial American," *William and Mary Quarterly 35* (Jan. 1978): 20-21.

5. Joan R. Gunderson and Gwen Victor Gampel, "Married Women's Legal Status in Eighteenth-Century New York and Virginia," *William and Mary Quarterly 39* (Jan. 1982): 27-29; Daniel Blake Smith, "The Study of the Family in Early America: Trends, Problems, and Prospects," *William and Mary Quarterly 39* (Jan. 1982): 15, 24; and Christopher Clark, "Household Economy, Market Exchange and the Rise of Capitalism in the Connecticut Valley, 1800-1860," *Journal of Social History 13* (1979): 169-90.

6. Daniel Snydacker, "Kinship and Community in Rural Pennsylvania," *Journal of Interdisciplinary History 13* (Summer 1982): 41-61.

7. Dennis P. Ryan, "Six Towns: Continuity and Change in Revolutionary New Jersey, 1770-1792," (Doctoral Dissertation, New York University, 1974) pp. 51-57; and Jerome H. Wood, Jr., "Conestega Crossroads: The Rise of Lancaster," *Pennsylvania*, 1730-1789,: (Doctoral Dissertation, Brown University, 1969), pp. 114-31.

8. Barry Levy, "Tender Plants: Quaker Farmers and Children in the Delaware Valley, 1681-1735," *Journal of Family History 3* (Summer 1978): 116-29.

9. Philip J. Greven Jr., *Four Generations: Population, Land, and Family in Colonial Andover, Massachusetts* (Ithaca: Cornell University Press, 1970), p. 251; and Snydacker, "Kinship and Community," p. 44.

10. Henretta, "Families and Farms," pp. 9, 12-15, 18-19, 28-29.

11. Daniel Scott Smith, "The Demographic History of Colonial New England," *The Journal of Economic History 32* (Mar. 1972): 165, 179-82; Ansley J. Coale and Melvin Zelnik, *New Estimates of Fertility and Population in the United States* (Princeton: Princeton University Press, 1963); Maris Vinovskis, *Fertility in Massachusetts from the Revolution to the Civil War* (New York: Academic Press, 1981); and Robert V. Wells, "Family Size and Fertility Control in Eighteenth-Century America: A Study of Quaker Families," *Population Studies 25* (Mar. 1971): 73-82.

12. Adam Smith, *An Inquiry into the Nature and Causes of the Wealth of Nations*, edited by C.J. Bullock (New York: P.F. Collier & Son, 1909), pp. 74-75.

13. Nancy R. Folbre, "The Wealth of Patriarchs: Deerfield, Massachusetts, 1760-1840," *Journal of Interdisciplinary History* 16 (Autumn 1985): 217-19; and Eva Mueller, "The Economic Value of Children in Peasant Agriculture," in Ronald G. Ridker, ed., *Population and Development: The Search for Selective Interventions* (Baltimore: The Johns Hopkins University Press, 1976), p. 146.

14. Henretta, "Families and Farms," p. 26; Greven, *Four Generations*, pp. 221, 253-58; and "Widowhood in Eighteenth Century Massachusetts: A Problem in the History of the Family," in Donald Fleming and Bernard Bailyn, eds., *Perspectives in American History. Volume 8*, (Cambridge, MA: Harvard University Press, 1974), pp. 83-119.

15. John E. Crowley, "The Importance of Kinship: Testamentary Evidence from South Carolina," *Journal of Interdisciplinary History* 16 (Spring 1986): 576-77; and Henretta, "Families and Farms," p. 32.

16. Folbre, "The Wealth of Patriarchs," p. 204-05.

17. Rollo Milton Tryon, *Household Manufacturers in the United States, 164-1860* (New York: A.M. Kelley. 1966, [Chicago, 1917 Rpt.]), pp. 243-76; and Paul G. Faler, "Workingmen, Mechanics and Social Change: Lynn Massachusetts, 1800-1860," (Doctoral Dissertation, University of Wisconsin, 1971).

18. Bertram Wyatt-Brown, "The Ideal Typology and Anti-bellum Southern History: A Testing of a New Approach," *Societas 5* (Winter 1975): 1-29; also George Fitzhugh, *Sociology for the South or the Failure of Free Society* (Richmond, VA: A. Morris, 1854).

19. *Ex Parte Crouse*, 4 Wharton Pa. 9 (1838).

20. *County of McLean v. Humphreys*, 104 Ill. 383 (1882).

21. Folbre, "Of Patriarchy Born," p. 213.

22. W.H. Hand, "The Need for Compulsory Education in the South." *The Child Labor Bulletin 1* (June 1912): 79.

23. *State v. Bailey*, 157 Ind. 324.

24. *Commonwealth v. Edsall*, 13 Pa. D.R. 509. See also: John Frederick Bender, *The Functions of Courts in Enforcing School Attendance Laws* (New York: Teachers College, Columbia University, 1927), pp. 10-19.

25. Katharine DuPre Lumpkin and Dorothy Wolff Douglas, *Child Workers in America* (New York: Robert M. McBride, 1937), pp. 86, 94-96, 236-37.

26. *Report to the President of the Committee on Economic Security* (Washington: U.S. Government Printing Office, 1935), pp. 23-25.

27. *Steward Machine Co. v. Davis*, 302 U.S. 548 (1937). See also: Robert Stevens, ed., *Statutory History of the United States: Income Security* (New York: Chelsea House Publishers, 1970), pp. 188-214.

28. Katherine Glover and Evelyn Dewey, *Children of the New Day* (New York: D. Appleton-Century Co., 1934), pp. 4-12, 183, 195, 200.

29. *Report to the President*, p. 36.

30. Lowell Gallaway and Richard Vedder, *Poverty, Income Distribution, the Family and Public Policy* (Washington: Joint Economic Committee, United States Congress, 1986), pp. 61-62.

31. *New Jersey Welfare Rights Organization v. Cahill*, 411 U.S. 619 (1973); and *King v. Smith*, 392 U.S. 309 (1968).

32. *Maynard v. Hill*, 125 U.S. 190, 210-211 (1888).

33. *Griswold v. Connecticut*, 381 U.S. 486 (1965).

34. *Eisenstadt v. Baird*, 495 U.S. 438, 543 (1972). On the general trend in recent Court decisions against marriage see: Carl Anderson, "The Supreme Court and the Economics of the Family," *The Family in America 1*, (Oct. 1987): 1-8.

35. See: Allan Carlson, "A Pro-Family Income Tax," *The Public Interest* 94 (Winter 1989): 69-75.

36. See: Allan Carlson, *Family Questions: Reflections on the American Social Crisis* (New Brunswick, NJ: Transactional Books, 1988): 257-72; Bryce Chrisensen, "The Costly Retreat From Marriage," *The Public Interest 91* (Spring 1988): 59-66; and Allan Carlson and Bryce Christensen, "Educational Content Within `The Bourgeois Family,'" Paper prepared for the Conference, *Education and Family*, held by the Office for Educational Research, U.S. Department of Education, June 1988.

37. Quoted in Levy, "Tender Plants," p. 117.

38. Carlson, *Family Questions*, pp. 171-181.

# The Constitution:
# Guarantor of Religion

## CHARLES E. RICE

The Constitution is a guarantor of religion in the sense that the more important of the religion clauses of the First Amendment aims to protect the free exercise of religious belief by all persons of whatever creed. The other clause, prohibiting laws "respecting an establishment of religion," was designed to be subordinate to the main objective of protecting the freedom of religious exercise. The system was well conceived and it worked effectively as long as the original purpose of both clauses was respected.

The religion clauses of the First Amendment provide: "Congress shall make no law respecting an establishment of religion, or prohibiting the free exercise thereof. . . ." The Supreme Court has held that these provisions bind the state and local governments as strictly as they bind Congress and the federal government. Litigation concerning the religion clauses is, to a considerable extent, a seasonal thing. In the springtime we have challenges to baccalaureate services and commencement invocations in public schools. When the weather turns cold, the attention shifts to the inclusion of nativity scenes in municipal "holiday" displays. Two recent cases illustrate the subtleties—some would say absurdities—of current litigation in this area.

In *Stein v. Plainwell Community Schools*,[1] a federal Court of Appeals acknowledged that invocations and benedictions at graduations could be constitutional as serving "the legitimate secular purposes of solemnizing public occasions, expressing confidence in the future, and encouraging the recognition of what is worthy of appreciation in society."[2] The invocations and benedictions in that case, however, were not "the 'civil' invocations or benedictions"[3] that would pass the secularity test. Rather, they were held unconstitutional because "they are framed and phrased so that they symbolically place the government's seal of approval on one religious view—the Christian view. They employ the language of Christian theology and prayer. Some expressly invoke the name of Jesus as the Savior."[4] The dissenting justice noted that

> had the speaker or leader at the time and place of the invocation read or led the audience in singing these words: "My Country 'Tis of Thee" or "Our Father's God to Thee, Author of Liberty," I doubt that this court, or any other, would find this activity unconstitutional. Had the speaker read, or guided the audience in a benediction with Irving Berlin's famous words, "God Bless America," or Julia Ward Howe's opening expression in the "Battle Hymn of the Republic" referring to the "glory of the Lord," again I doubt any finding of constitutional offense. These words in favorite songs, used at innumerable public ceremonies, including graduation ceremonies, contain plain and repeated reference to the Deity and ask His Blessing or give thanks for His guidance and assistance. They are both a form of invocation and benediction which in content is known in advance; yet they do not violate the first amendment. The remarks used to open and close the ceremonies in this case are no more violative of the constitution than are these expressions referring to the Deity.[5]

In 1984, the Supreme Court held that the inclusion by

Pawtucket, Rhode Island, of a Nativity creche in its downtown holiday display did not violate the First Amendment.[6] The Pawtucket display included "among other things, a Santa Claus house, reindeer pulling Santa's sleigh, candy-striped poles, a Christmas tree, carolers, cutout figures representing such characters as a clown, an elephant, and a teddy bear, hundreds of colored lights, a large banner that reads, 'Season's Greetings' and the creche at issue here. All components of this display are owned by the city."[7] The 5-4 majority of the Supreme Court held that there was insufficient evidence "that the inclusion of the creche is a purposeful or surreptitious effort to express some kind of subtle governmental advocacy of a particular religious message. In a pluralistic society a variety of motives and purposes are implicated. The city, like the Congresses and Presidents, however, has principally taken note of a significant historical religious event long celebrated in the Western World. The creche in the display depicts the historical origins of this traditional event long recognized as a national holiday."[8] Even if part of the motivation for the creche were religious, the Court concluded that "the city has a secular purpose for including the creche"[9] and held that the existence of that secular purpose satisfies the Supreme Court's criteria. Nor was the display rendered unconstitutional by the fact that it indirectly or incidentally advanced religion: "The display engenders a friendly community spirit of good will in keeping with the [Christmas] season."[10]

The Court majority upheld this "inclusion of a single symbol of a particular historic religious event, as part of a celebration acknowledged in the Western World for 20 centuries, and in this country by the people, by the Executive Branch, by the Congress and the courts for two centuries."[11] Nevertheless, as Justice Brennan aptly observed in dissent, "it remains uncertain whether absent such secular symbols as Santa Claus' house, a talking wishing well, and cut-out clowns and bears, a similar nativity scene would pass muster under the Court's standard."[12] The creche was allowed, but at the price of its reduction to triviality. "The creche has been relegated," wrote Justice Blackmun in dissent, "to the role of a neutral harbinger of the holiday season, useful for commercial purposes, but devoid of any inherent meaning and incapable of enhancing the religious tenor of a display of which it is an integral part. The city has its victory— but it is a Pyrrhic one indeed."[13]

The reasoning of the Supreme Court in cases involving religious observances is far removed from the evident intent of the First Congress and of the states that ratified the First Amendment. The original intent of the Establishment Clause of the First Amendment, as described by Professor Edward S. Corwin, was that "Congress should not prescribe a national faith, a possibility which those states with establishments of their own—Massachusetts, New Hampshire, Connecticut, Maryland, and South Carolina—probably regarded with fully as much concern as those which had gotten rid of their establishment."[14] The intent of the Establishment Clause to permit government to encourage religion—and especially Christianity—was confirmed by Justice Joseph Story, who served as a Justice of the Supreme Court from 1811 to 1845 and who was a leading Unitarian:

> Probably at the time of the adoption of the constitution, and of the first amendment to it . . ., the general, if not the universal sentiment in America was, that Christianity ought to receive encouragement from the state, so far as was not incompatible with the private rights of conscience, and the freedom of religious worship. An attempt to level all religions, and to make it a matter of state policy to hold all in utter indifference, would have created universal disapprobation if not universal indignation.
>
> The real object of the amendment was, not to countenance, much less to advance Mohammed–anism, or

Judaism, or infidelity, by prostrating Christianity; but to exclude all rivalry among Christian sects, and to prevent any national ecclesiastical establishment which should give to a hierarchy the exclusive patronage of the national government.[15]

The view of the Supreme Court today, which forbids even the posting of the Ten Commandments in public schools,[16] would have been utterly rejected by the framers of the First Amendment. The Northwest Ordinance, adopted by the Constitutional Congress in 1787, provided public support for religious education: "Religion, morality, and knowledge, being necessary to good government and the happiness of mankind, schools and the means of learning, shall forever be encouraged." This enactment was reaffirmed by Congress in 1789. After the new constitution was ratified, the First Congress, on September 24-26, 1789, did two things. They approved, and sent to the states for ratification, the First Amendment. And they called on President Washington to "recommend to the people of the United States a day of public thanksgiving and prayer, to be observed by acknowledging, with grateful hearts, the many signal favors of Almighty God. . . ." Can you believe that the Congress intended the First Amendment to forbid the sort of prayer it recommended on the same day? Nor was this a result of inadvertence. Representative Thomas Tucker of South Carolina objected that the call for a day of prayer "is a religious matter, and, as such, is proscribed to us."[17] Congress passed the resolution, thus overriding with full awareness the argument the Supreme Court has adopted as doctrine today.

Religion was generally seen as necessary to the promotion of civic virtue. The role of government as a promoter of theistic belief was widely accepted, as can be surmised from George Washington's Farewell Address:

Of all the dispositions and habits which lead to political prosperity, religion and morality are indispensable supports. In vain would that man claim the tribute of patriotism who should labor to subvert these great pillars of human happiness, these firmest props of the duties of men and citizens. The mere politician, equally with the pious man, ought to respect and to cherish them. A volume could not trace all their connections with private and public felicity. Let it simply be asked where is the security for property, for reputation, for life, if the sense of religious obligation desert the oaths, which are the instrument of investigation in courts of justice? And let us with caution indulge the supposition that morality can be maintained without religion. Whatever may be conceded to the influence of refined education on minds of peculiar structure, reason and experience both forbid us to expect that national morality can prevail in exclusion of religious principle.[18]

There is abundant evidence that the original constitutional posture of the government of the United States with respect to religion was one of generalized promotion of Christianity or at least of theism, while protecting the free exercise of religion of all, whether believers or not. In 1844, the Supreme Court of the United States observed:

It is also said, and truly, that the Christian religion is a part of the common law of Pennsylvania . . . in this qualified sense, that its divine origin and truth are admitted, and therefore it is not to be maliciously and openly reviled and blasphemed against, to the annoyance of believers or the injury of the public . . . .[19]

In the case of *Holy Trinity Church v. United States*,[20] the Supreme Court unanimously held that a congressional statute prohibiting the immigration of persons under contract to perform labor did not apply to an English minister who entered this country under a contract to preach at a New York church. The Court recited the legislative history of the act and then said:

> But beyond all these matters no purpose of action against religion can be imputed to any legislation, state or national, because this is a religious people. This is historically true. From the discovery of this continent to the present hour, there is a single voice making this affirmation . . . .
>
> . . . If we pass beyond these matters to a view of American life as expressed by its laws, its business, its customs and its society, we find everywhere a clear recognition of the same truth . . . . These, and many other matters which might be noticed, add a volume of unofficial declarations to the mass of organic utterances that this is a Christian nation.[21]

The American system worked well as long as the people generally adhered to Christianity and as long as they recognized the general Christian principles of natural law as implicit elements of the Constitution. But the American Christian consensus eroded. In the 1963 decision which outlawed prayer in public schools, Justice William Brennan aptly said:

> [O]ur religious composition makes us a vastly more diverse people than were our forefathers. They knew differences chiefly among Protestant sects. Today the Nation is far more heterogeneous religiously, including as it does substantial minorities not only of Catholics and Jews but as well of those who worship according to no version of the Bible and those who worship no God at all.[22]

As the American religious consensus changed, so, too, did the posture of government toward religion. The Supreme Court in recent years has interpreted the Establishment Clause to require not merely neutrality on the part of government among Christian and other theistic sects, but neutrality between theism and non-theism.[23] It is impossible, however, for government to maintain neutrality on the existence of God. To affirm God is a preference of theism; to deny Him a preference of atheism; and to suspend judgement a preference of agnosticism which is itself a religion. In *Torcaso v. Watkins*,[24] the Supreme Court held unconstitutional a requirement in the Constitution of Maryland that state employees declare their belief in God. The requirement, said the Court, was unconstitutional because "the power and authority of the State of Maryland thus is put on the side of one particular sort of believers—those who are willing to say they believe in 'the existence of God.'"[25] Neither state nor federal government, said the Court, "can aid those religions based on a belief in the existence of God as against those religions founded on different beliefs."[26] A footnote to this statement asserted that, "Among religions in this country which do not teach what would commonly be considered a belief in the custom of God are Buddhism, Taoism, Ethical Culture, Secular Humanism and others."[27]

The Court requires government at all levels to maintain a neutrality between theism and non-theism which results, in practical effect, in a governmental preference of the religion of agnostic secularism. Justice Brennan argued, in his concurrence in the 1963 school prayer case, that the words "under God" could still be kept in the Pledge of Allegiance only because they "no longer have a religious purpose or meaning." Instead, according to Brennan they "may merely recognize the historical fact that our Nation was believed to have been founded 'under God.'"[28] This false neutrality would logically prevent an assertion by any government official, whether President or school teacher, that the Declaration of Independence—the first of the Organic Laws of the United States printed at the head of the United States Code—is in fact true when it asserts that men are endowed "by their Creator" with certain unalienable rights and when it affirms "the Laws of Nature and of Nature's God," a "Supreme Judge of the world" and "Divine Providence." If a pupil asks his public school teacher whether God exists, as the Declaration affirms He does, and if the teacher says, "Yes," that is unconstitutional as a preference of theism; if the teacher says, "No," that is unconstitutional as a preference of atheism. The only thing the teacher can do, according to the theory of the Court, is to suspend judgment, to say, "I (the State) do not know." But this is an affirmation of the religion of agnosticism.

The operation of this Supreme Court version of the Establishment Clause can be seen in *Smith v. Board of School Com'rs of Mobile County*,[29] where Federal District Judge W. Brevard Hand held that the use of certain home economics, history, and social studies textbooks in public schools violated the Establishment Clause of the First Amendment because the use of the books had the primary effect of advancing the religion of secular humanism. In an earlier phase of the case, Judge Hand said, "It was pointed out in the testimony that the curriculum on the public schools of Mobile County is rife with efforts at teaching or encouraging secular humanism—all without opposition from any other ethic— to such an extent that it becomes a brainwashing effort. If this Court is compelled to purge 'God is great, God is good, we thank him for our daily food' from the classroom, then this Court must also purge from the classroom those things that serve to teach that salvation is through one's self rather than through a deity."[30]

In his opinion in the *Smith* case, Judge Hand spelled out the criteria by which he concluded that the public schools were in fact promoting a secular religion:

> The question arises how public schools can deal with topics that overlap with areas covered by religious belief. Mere coincidence between a statement in a textbook and a religious belief is not an establishment

of religion. However, some religious beliefs are so fundamental that the act of denying them will completely undermine that religion. In addition, denial of *that* belief will result in the affirmance of a contrary belief and result in the establishment of an opposing religion.

The state may teach that lying is wrong, as a social and civil regulation, but if, in so doing it advances a reason for the rule, the possible different reasons must be explained evenhandedly. As otherwise stated, the state may not promote one particular reason over another in the public schools.

Teaching that moral choices are purely personal and can only be based on some autonomous, as yet undiscovered and unfulfilled, inner self is a sweeping fundamental belief that must not be promoted by the public schools. The state can, of course, teach the law of the land, which is that each person is responsible for, and will be held to account for, his actions.[31]

As one commentator noted, "The textbooks in the Alabama dispute won't even say why the pilgrims came to this country, or who it was that they gave thanks to on the first Thanksgiving. 'All the [Alabama] case is trying to do is get the facts about religion back in the textbooks,' says Thomas F. Parker, the lawyer for the parents. 'When you exclude religion, you're belittling religion.' William Bradford, a lawyer defending the school board, doesn't dispute this diagnosis, but says: 'Bad history is not a constitutional violation.'"[32]

Not surprisingly, Judge Hand was reversed by the Court of Appeals, which stated,

The Supreme Court has never established a comprehensive test for determining the 'delicate question' of

what constitutes a religious belief for purposes of the
first amendment, and we need not attempt to do so in
this case, for we find that, even assuming that secular
humanism is a religion for purposes of the establishment clause, Appellees have failed to prove a violation
of the establishment clause through the use in the
Alabama public schools of the textbooks at issue in this
case. The religion clauses of the first amendment
require that states "pursue a course of complete neutrality toward religion" . . . . The Supreme Court has
developed three criteria to serve as guidelines in determining whether this barrier has been breached by
challenged government action: first, the statute must
have a secular legislative purpose; second, its principal
or primary effect must be one that neither advances
nor inhibits religion; finally, the statute must not
foster 'an excessive government entanglement with
religion.' *Lemon v. Kurtzman* . . . . Governmental action violates the establishment clause if it fails to meet
any of these three criteria . . . . Although the Supreme
Court occasionally has decided establishment cases
without utilizing the *Lemon* criteria . . . the Supreme
Court recently reaffirmed the vitality of the *Lemon*
test, noting that the Court has 'particularly relied on
*Lemon* in every case involving the sensitive relationship between government and religion in the eduction
of our children . . . ."[33]

The *Smith* case turned on the "effect" prong of the Lemon test,
and the Court of Appeals held that Judge Hand was wrong in
concluding that the challenged textbooks both advanced secular
humanism and inhibited theistic religion. Rather, the Court of
Appeals held that the "use of the challenged textbooks has the
primary effect of conveying information that is essentially neutral in its religious content to the school children who utilize the

books; none of these books convey a message of governmental approval of secular humanism or governmental disapproval of theism."[34]

Generations of public school children, however, have passed through the system in the past quarter-century without ever seeing the State, in the person of their teachers, acknowledge that there is a standard of right and wrong higher than the State and that "the Laws of Nature and of Nature's God" are in fact a limit on the power of the State. Moreover, the false rule of neutrality requires that public schools must treat sensitive moral issues such as homosexual activity, promiscuity, abortion, etc., in a "non-judgmental" manner that cannot help but inculcate a relativistic attitude in the students. One result is a potential abridgment of the free exercise of religion of students who do not subscribe to the secular orthodoxy. In *Mozert v. Hawkins County Board of Education*,[35] Christian parents and children objected to a public school requirement that their children use the Holt, Rinehart and Winston basic reading series which in various respects was offensive to Christian belief. "The district court held that the plaintiffs' free exercise rights have been burdened because their 'religious beliefs compel them to refrain from *exposure* to the Holt series,' and the defendant school board 'has effectively required that the student plaintiffs either read the offensive texts or give up their free public education.'"[36] The district court entered an injunction prohibiting the defendants "from requiring the student-plaintiffs to read from the Holt series," and ordering the defendants to excuse the student plaintiffs from their classrooms "[d]uring the normal reading period" and to provide them with suitable space in the library or elsewhere for a study hall.[37] The Court of Appeals reversed and ordered that the complaint be dismissed:

> The Supreme Court has recently affirmed that public schools serve the purpose of teaching fundamental

values "essential to a democratic society." These values "include tolerance of divergent political and religious views" while taking into account "consideration of the sensibilities of others . . . ." The Court has noted with apparent approval the view of some educators who see public schools as an "assimilative force" that brings together "diverse and conflicting elements" in our society "on a broad but common ground . . . ." The critical reading approach furthers these goals. Mrs. Frost stated specifically that she objected to stories that develop "a religious tolerance that all religions are merely different roads to God." Stating that the plaintiffs reject this concept, presented as a recipe for an ideal world citizen, Mrs. Frost said, "We cannot be tolerant in that we accept other religious views on an equal basis with ours." While probably not an uncommon view of true believers in any religion, this statement graphically illustrates what is lacking in the plaintiff's case.

The "tolerance of divergent . . . religious views" referred to by the Supreme Court is a civil tolerance, not a religious one. It does not require a person to accept any other religion as the equal of the one to which that person adheres. It merely requires a recognition that in a pluralistic society we must "live and let live." If the Hawkins County schools had required the plaintiff students either to believe or say they believe that "all religions are merely different roads to God," this would be a different case. No instrument of government can, consistent with the Free Exercise Clause, require such a belief of affirmation. However, there was absolutely no showing that the defendant school board sought to do this; indeed, the school board agreed at oral argument that it could not constitutionally do so.[38]

Over the past few years, public schools have increasingly stressed the teaching of a common core of "values," such as honesty, respect for others, etc. Even People for the American Way and Americans United for Separation of State have called for increased teaching about religion in public schools.

> Educators cite numerous reasons for the new interest in values, beginning with anxiety about widely publicized problems like drugs and teen-age pregnancy. "People are afraid that the moral fiber of the country is falling apart," said Mary Hatwood Futrell, the president of National Education Association. "They turn to the schools to do something about it." Others see the trend toward more explicit teaching of values as part of a much broader reaction. "The pendulum is swinging back from the romantic idea of the 60s that all societal values are oppressive and that the only thing that counts is the individual," said Bill Honig, the Superintendent of Public Instruction in California. "Educators went along with all this craziness, so we've ended up with students who are ethically illiterate . . . ." "Look at the values of the Constitution," said Scott Thomson, the executive director of the National Association of Secondary School Principals. "They are rooted in the secular notion that man is a creature of reason and can govern himself, but also in the religious notion that men are equal because they are created by God."[39]

A satisfactory solution, however, cannot be found in the promotion of lowest common denominator "values." Rather, the solution should begin with the recognition that, in Alfred North Whitehead's words, "The essence of education is that it be religious."[40] If elementary and secondary education truly has an inherent religious character, a serious question is presented as to the legitimacy of state-conducted public education itself in light of the establishment and free exercise clauses of the First Amendment: If education is intrinsically religious, how could the state's assumption of the role of educator be consistent with the neutrality mandate of the establishment clause as presently interpreted?

"The statist educators," in the words of Rev. R. J. Rushdoony, "have indeed controlled America's future by controlling its schools; they have made the curriculum of those schools more and more openly humanistic and anti-Christian."[41] Dr. Rushdoony's point was echoed on the other side by a writer in *The American Atheist*:

> And how does a god die? Quite simply because all his religionists have been converted to another religion, and there is no one left to make children believe they need him.
>
> Finally, it is irresistible—we must ask how we can kill the god of Christianity. We need only insure that our schools teach only secular knowledge; that they teach children to constantly examine and question all theories and truths put before them in any form; and that they teach that nothing is proven by the number of persons who believe a thing to be true. If we could achieve this, god would indeed be shortly due for a funeral service.[42]

At the same time that it has purged theistic influence from public life and especially from public schools, the Supreme Court has made life difficult for religious institutions by interpreting the three-part *Lemon* test in contradictory and bizarre ways. As Justice Rehnquist noted in his dissent in *Wallace v. Jaffree* in 1985:

For example, a State may lend to parochial school-children geography textbooks that contain maps of the United States, but the State may not lend maps of the United States for use in geography class. A State may lend textbooks on American colonial history, but it may not lend a film on George Washington, or a film projector to show it in history class. A State may lend classroom workbooks, but may not lend workbooks in which the parochial school-children write, thus rendering them nonreusable. A State may pay for bus transportation to religious schools, but may not pay for bus transportation from the parochial school to the public zoo or natural history museum for a field trip. A State may pay for diagnostic services conducted in the parochial school but therapeutic services must be given in a different building; speech and hearing "services" conducted by the State inside the sectarian school are forbidden . . . but the State may conduct speech and hearing diagnostic tests inside the sectarian school . . . . Exceptional parochial school students may receive counselling, but it must take place outside of the parochial school, such as in a trailer parked down the street . . . . A State may give cash to a parochial school to pay for the administration of state-written tests and state-ordered reporting services, but it may not provide funds for teacher-prepared tests on secular subjects. Religious instruction may not be given in public school, but the public school may release students during the day for religion classes elsewhere, and may enforce attendance at those classes with its truancy laws.[43]

No one could seriously argue that the results cited by Justice Rehnquist are consistent. Nor could it be maintained that such freakish nit-picking is consistent with the grand—and essentially simple—design of those who wrote and adopted the First

Amendment. The religion clauses of that amendment ensured governmental neutrality as among religious sects while permitting governmental encouragement of belief in God. The founders recognized that the state cannot be neutral on the basic question of the existence of God. The Supreme Court reminds us of that reality through the effect of its decisions in imposing on the people a governmental preference of the religion which is agnostic secular humanism. In the process, government is compelled by the Court to act in a manner hostile to theistic—especially to Christian—beliefs and organizations. For example, in April, 1987, Federal District Judge Charles B. Richey held unconstitutional the Adolescent Family Life Act (AFLA) of 1981. The Act provided funds to furnish counseling and other services to pregnant adolescents and it required applicants to involve, "as appropriate in the provision of services . . . religious and charitable organizations, voluntary associations, and other groups in the private sector as well as services provided by publicly sponsored initiatives . . . ."[44] Judge Richey held that the Act "has the primary effect of advancing religion because it funds teaching and counseling of adolescents by religious organizations on matters related to religious doctrine."[45] Moreover, he ruled, "the risk that AFLA funds will be used to transmit religious doctrine can be overcome only by government monitoring so continuous that it rises to the level of excessive entanglement."[46]

Judge Richey's decision has been accepted for review by the Supreme Court.[47] The case is significant because it represents an application of the Supreme Court's view that, in Judge Richey's words, a program "violates a core purpose of the Establishment Clause if it conveys a message of government endorsement of religion in general or of a particular religion that benefits from government largesse . . . ."[48] This prohibition of governmental endorsement not only "of a particular religion" but also of "religion in general" relegates adherents of some theistic religions to a status of second class citizenship. Adherents of nontheistic, secular beliefs can participate freely in the AFLA program. So can theists who accept premarital sex and abortion. The only persons who cannot participate are theists who regard premarital sex and abortion as wrong. "It is a fundamental tenet of many religions that premarital sex and abortion are wrong, even sinful . . . . The AFLA does not prohibit these religions from receiving AFLA grants. Thus, by contemplating the provision of aid to organizations affiliated with these religions—aid for the purpose of encouraging abstinence and adoption—the AFLA contemplates subsidizing a fundamental religious mission of those organizations."[49] As columnist Cal Thomas noted,

> The point is that portions of the act permitting counseling by church groups work better than any other formula that has been tried. The proof was right under Judge Richey's nose. The case involved Catholic Charities of Arlington, Virginia, which at the time the suit was filed by the American Civil Liberties Union had received $75,000 for a pregnancy-prevention program. The program was made available not only to parochial schools but to the entire community. Betty West, director of Children's Services for Catholic Charities, told me that of the 250 pregnant young women they counseled annually, "only three or four" ever returned with unwanted pregnancies after going through the program. Though it was impossible to follow up on every case, she added that of those who kept in contact, the vast majority were leading responsible lives. "One girl who came to us had had four abortions," she said. "She was pregnant with a fifth child. We gave her counseling and she had the baby. Today she is working and supporting herself and her baby. We helped her find God and she joined a prayer group which has given her great support." Betty West says this is a typical example. If non-religious pro-

grams have failed the young woman four times, why should anyone object when a religiously based program succeeds? Is the goal to help people or to discriminate against religion?[50]

Perhaps the major lesson to be drawn here is that there is no such thing as a free lunch and that the churches would be better off without any sort of government aid. The state has the right to regulate that which it subsidizes. The churches would be better off if they rejected government grants, loans and other forms of subsidy. The Supreme Court has even interpreted the religious exemption from taxation as a form of subsidy that subjects the church to controls according to Congress' varying notions of public policy.[51] The basis for the tax exemption of churches is one of dominion, that the state is inherently without jurisdiction to tax the religious activities of the church. While the tax exemption of churches is legitimate, it ought not to be regarded as a subsidy. And government subsidies, whether by grant, loan, or otherwise, should be rejected.

The Supreme Court's erroneous interpretations of the Establishment Clause have institutionalized a governmental preference of agnostic secularism as the official national creed. This error has been compounded by the Supreme Court's misinterpretation of the Fourteenth Amendment so as to bind the state and local governments strictly by the Court's interpretation of the Bill of Rights.

The Bill of Rights was originally intended to preserve the rights enumerated therein against infringement by the national government. State constitutions, enforced by state courts, were relied upon for the protection of personal liberties against abuse by state governments. The states generally had constitutional provisions corresponding to the Bill of Rights; but federalism itself was regarded by the Framers as such an essential bulwark of liberty that even where states did not have such provisions, the Bill of Rights still did not apply to the states. Thus, the Supreme

Court in *Barron v. Baltimore*[52] declared that the prohibitions in the Bill of Rights were intended solely to limit the powers of the federal government and did not bind the states.

The Fourteenth Amendment, adopted in 1868, prohibited the states from abridging the privileges and immunities of citizens of the United States, depriving any person of life, liberty, or property without due process of law and denying to any person the equal protection of the laws. The legislative history of the Amendment and the records of the ratifying states indicate that neither Congress nor the states intended that the Amendment would apply the Bill of Rights as a further restriction on the power of the states. Charles Fairman, in a definitive article, assembled a "mountain of evidence" from the congressional debates, the state ratifying proceedings and other original sources in support of his conclusion that the framers and ratifiers of the Fourteenth Amendment did not intend to make the Bill of Rights applicable against the states. He contrasted this "mountain of evidence" with "the few stones and pebbles that made up the theory that the Fourteenth Amendment incorporated Amendments I to VIII."[53] Several court decisions following the Fourteenth Amendment's ratification also showed the contemporary understanding that the Amendment did not require compliance with the Bill of Rights. This is especially true of the Establishment Clause. The Supreme Court of New Hampshire, for example, only months after the Amendment was ratified, emphasized that "the whole power over the subject of religion is left exclusively to the state governments," and was unaffected by the Fourteenth Amendment.[54] The Supreme Court, however, has now interpreted the Fourteenth Amendment to incorporate the Bill of Rights so as to require the states to comply with virtually every provision of the Bill of Rights, including the Establishment Clause. One effect of the Supreme Court's incorporation doctrine has been "to broaden the Fourteenth Amendment and curtail States' Rights beyond the wildest conceptions of the framers and ratifiers."[55] This expansive interpretation of due process has resulted in a greater role for the federal judiciary and has altered the balance of power between the federal and state governments. Personal rights are now chiefly under the protection of the United States Constitution, as defined by the Supreme Court, rather than under the protection of the state constitutions. Moreover, the Court has extended the notion of due process under the Fourteenth Amendment to embrace "fundamental rights" not found in the Constitution itself. Thus, in *Griswold v. Connecticut*,[56] the Court found a right of reproductive privacy in "penumbras formed by emanations from" the Bill of Rights. This right was thereafter extended to prevent the states from prohibiting abortion.[57] Through its application of the Bill of Rights strictly against the states, the Supreme Court has claimed for itself the power to determine the meaning and application of virtually all personal and civil rights. The effect of this inventive jurisprudence is nowhere more evident than with respect to the religion clauses of the First Amendment.

Apart from the fact that the framers of the Fourteenth Amendment never intended to apply any of the first eight amendments against the states, there are special reasons why the Establishment Clause is uniquely unsuited for incorporation in the Fourteenth Amendment. The other provisions of the first eight amendments—*e.g.*, against unreasonable searches and seizures, self-incrimination, etc.—are protections of specific personal liberties against infringement by the government of the United States. Even if it were true that the Fourteenth Amendment was intended to protect those liberties against infringement by the states, it would be unsound to draw that conclusion with respect to the Establishment Clause. For the Establishment Clause was not intended to prevent government from encouraging religion and morality by acknowledging God. Rather, it was primarily intended to exclude the federal government entirely from legislating in any direction on the subject of establishments of religion and to ensure that the subject would be exclusively and unrestrictedly within the competence of the state governments. In 1845, the Supreme Court said, "The Constitution makes no provision for protecting the citizens of the respective states in their religious liberties; this is left to the state constitutions and laws. Nor is there any inhibition imposed by the constitution in this respect on the states."[58] The "principal importance" of the Establishment Clause, wrote Edward S. Corwin, "lay in the separation which it effected between the respective jurisdictions of State and nation regarding religion, rather than in its bearing on the question of the Separation of Church and State."[59] The Establishment Clause was intended not as a protection of personal liberty but as a delineation of federal and state jurisdiction. It is therefore unsound for the Supreme Court to hold that the Establishment Clause is applied against the states by the provision of the Fourteenth Amendment which forbids the states to deprive any person of "liberty" without due process of law.

With the replacement of retired Justice Lewis Powell by Justice Anthony Kennedy, we may see interpretations of the Establishment Clause which are more faithful to the original meaning of that provision. The problem, however, is bigger than devising adjustments in the *Lemon* test. It requires a repudiation of the secularist view of the Establishment Clause. And it requires a repudiation of the incorporation doctrine by which the Supreme Court's interpretation of the Bill of Rights have been fastened uniformly on every state and local government in the land. The genius of the Constitution was that it left such issues as religion to the states and the people. But as long as the subject of religion is committed instead to the edicts of nine unelected judges, the temptation will ultimately prove irresistible for those judges to become what Judge Learned Hand called "a bevy of Platonic guardians."[60]

## ENDNOTES

1. 822 F.2d 1406 (6th Cir., 1987).

2. 822 F.2d at 1409.

3. 822 F.2d at 1410.

4. 822 F.2d at 1410.

5. 822 F.2d at 1417.

6. *Lynch v. Donnelly*, 465 U.S. 668 (1984).

7. 465 U.S. at 681.

8. 465 U.S. at 680.

9. 465 U.S. at 685.

10. 465 U.S. at 685.

11. 465 U.S. at 686.

12. 465 U.S. at 695, n.1.

13. 465 U.S. at 727.

14. Edward Samuel Corwin, *The Powers in a Secular State* (1951), 102, 106.

15. Joseph Story, *Commentaries on the Constitution of the United States* (3rd ed., Boston: Hilliard, Gray, 1858), 2 Secs. 1874, 1877.

16. *Stone v. Graham*, 449 U.S. 39 (1980).

17. Annals of Cong. 915 (1789-91).

18. W. David Stedman & LaVaughn G. Lewis (eds.) *Our Ageless Constitution* (Evanston, IL: Stedman & Associates, 1987).

19. *Vidal v. Girard's Executors*, 43 U.S. 126, 198 (1844).

20. 143 U.S. 457, 470-71 (1892).

21. *Ibid.*

22. *Abington School District v. Schempp*, 374 U.S. 203 239-40 (1963).

23. See *Torcaso v. Watkins*, 367 U.S. 488 (1961); *Abington School District v. Schempp*, 374 U.S. 203 (1963).

24. 367 U.S. 488 (1961).

25. 367 U.S. at 490.

26. 367 U.S. at 495.

27. 367 U.S. at 495.

28. *Abington School District v. Schempp*, 374 U.S. 203, 304, (1963).

29. 655 F. Supp. 939, 987 (S.D. Ala. 1987).

30. *Jaffree v. Board of School Com'rs of Mobile County.* 554 F. Supp. 1104, 1129, n.41 (S.D. Ala. 1983).

31. 655 F. Supp. at 987 (emphasis in original).

32. Suzanne Fields, "Reading the Buzz Words," *Washington Times*, October 14, 1986,

p. D1, col. 5.

33. *Smith v. Board of School Com'rs of Mobile County*, 827 F.2d at 684, 689 (11th Cir. 1987) (citations omitted).

34. 827 F.2d at 690.

35. 827 F.2d 1058 (6th Cir., 1987).

36. 827 F.2d at 1062 (emphasis in original).

37. 927 F.2d at 1063.

38. 827 F.2d at 1068-69.

39. *N.Y. Times*, Sep. 15, 1986, p.1, col. 3.

40. Alfred North Whitehead, *The Aims of Education* (New York: Free Press, 1967), 25.

41. R.J. Rushdoony, Introduction to A. Grover, *Ohio's Trojan Horse* (1977), 6.

42. Bozarth, On Keeping God Alive, *Am. Atheist*, Nov. 1977, at 7,8.

43. *Wallace v. Jaffree*, 472 U.S. 38, 110-11 (1985).

44. *Kendrick v. Bowen*, 657 F. Supp. 1547, 1553 (D.C. Dist. Col., 1987).

45. 657 F. Supp. at 1562.

46. 657 F. Supp. at 1567.

47. *Bowen v. Kendrick*, 108 S. Ct. 326 (1987).

48. 657 F. Supp. at 1561.

49. 657 F. Supp. at 1563 (citations omitted).

50. Cal Thomas, "Success Formula Rejected," *Washington Times*, Apr. 23, 1967, p. 3D, col. 6.

51. *Bob Jones Univ. v. U.S.*, 461 U.S. 574 (1983).

52. 32 U.S. (7 Pet) 243 (1833).

53. Fairman, "Does the Fourteenth Amendment Incorporate the Bill of Rights," 2 *Stanford Law Review* 5 (1949).

54. *Hale v. Everett*, 53 N.H. 1, 124 (1868).

55. Raoul Berger, *Government by Judiciary: The Transformation of the Fourteenth Amendment.* (Cambridge: Harvard University Press, 1977), p. 36, n.95.

56. 381 U.S. 479, 484 (1965).

57. *Roe v. Wade*, 410 U.S. 113 (1973).

58. *Permoli v. First Municipality of New Orleans*, 44 U.S. 588, 609 (1845).

59. Edward Samuel Corwin, The Supreme Court as National School Board, in *A Constitution of Powers in a Secular State* (1951), 106.

60. Hand, *The Bill of Rights* (1958), 73.

# About the Contributors

*William B. Allen* is Dean of James Madison College at Michigan State University. Previously Professor of Government at Harvey Mudd College, Dean Allen is the author of numerous essays on the Founding and other subjects, most notably on George Washington and the *Federalist Papers*. He edited *George Washington: A Collection*, and authored *Dateline 1787: A Curriculum Package*.

*Pasco M. Bowman* was appointed to the United States Court of Appeals for the Eighth Circuit by President Reagan on July 19, 1983. Previously, he was dean and professor at the University of Missouri-Kansas City School of Law from July 1979 to July 1983; visiting professor of law at the University of Virginia from 1978 to 1979; from 1970 to 1978 was dean and professor of law at Wake Forest; and from 1960 to 1964 he was on the faculty of law at the University of Georgia. Judge Bowman was a Root-Tilden scholar at New York University School of Law where he received his J.D. in 1958. He completed his LL.M. at the University of Virginia in 1986, and was awarded an honorary LL.D. in 1988 by Bridgewater College.

*Allan C. Carlson* has been President of The Rockford Institute in Illinois since 1986. In 1988, he was appointed by President Reagan to serve as a member of the National Commission on Children, on which he served through 1991. Dr. Carlson has written extensively on the subjects of modern social history, family, policy, the relationship between foreign and domestic policies, the interaction of economics and culture, and modern religion. His books include *Family Questions: Reflections on the American Social Crisis* and *The Swedish Experiment in Family*

*Politics: The Myrdals and the Interwar Population Crisis.* Dr. Carlson received his Ph.D. in Modern European History from Ohio University.

*The Honorable Robert T. Donnelly* took office as a judge on the Supreme Court of the State of Missouri on September 7, 1965, and served until retirement on January 1, 1989. Justice Donnelly was Chief Justice of the Supreme Court of the State of Missouri from 1973 to 1975 and from 1981 to 1983.

*William F. Harvey* is the Carl M. Gray Professor of Law and Advocacy at Indiana University. He is the author of seventeen volumes published by West Publishing Company. He has received six awards for outstanding teaching. Professor Harvey has participated in several major cases in trial and appellate courts and in the United States Supreme Court. He received his J.D. and LL.M. degrees from Georgetown University, and his A.B. degree from the University of Missouri.

*Forrest McDonald*, Distinguished Research Professor of History at the University of Alabama, was the Sixteenth Jefferson Lecturer in the Humanities in 1987. He was awarded the Ingersoll Prize in 1990, and the ISI Henry Salvatori Prize in 1994. Professor McDonald is the author of several books including *Novus Ordo Seclorum* and his most recent book is *The American Presidency: An Intellectual History.*

*Edward B. McLean* holds the Eugene N. and Marian C. Beesley Chair in Political Science at Wabash College. He has served eighteen years as Deputy Prosecutor in Montgomery County, Indiana. Professor McLean received his J.D. and Ph.D. degrees from Indiana University. He recently published *Law and Civilization: The Legal Thought of Roscoe Pound.*

*Richard Neely* is a Justice of the West Virginia Supreme Court of Appeals and a graduate of Dartmouth College and Yale Law School. Justice Neely has served three terms as Chief Justice of West Virginia, and is the author of six books, including *How Courts Govern America* (Yale Press, 1980) and *The Product Liability Mess* (The Free Press, 1989).

*Charles Rice* is Professor of Law at the University of Notre Dame. He is co-editor of The American Journal of Jurisprudence. Professor Rice has published widely in the area of Constitutional Law and Natural Law. His most recent book is *Fifty Questions on the Natural Law.*